The Servant Problem

The Servant Problem
Domestic Employment in a Global Economy

Rosie Cox

I.B. TAURIS
LONDON · NEW YORK

Published in 2006 by I.B. Tauris & Co Ltd

6 Salem Road   175 Fifth Avenue
London W2 4BU   New York NY 10010

www.ibtauris.com

In the United States of America and Canada distributed by
Palgrave Macmillan a division of St. Martin's Press
175 Fifth Avenue, New York NY 10010

ISBN: 1 85043 619 3 HB
EAN: 978 1 85043 619 5 HB

ISBN: 1 85043 620 7 PB
EAN: 978 1 85043 620 1 PB

A full CIP record for this book is available from the British Library
A full CIP record is available from the Library of Congress

Library of Congress Catalog Card Number: available

Typeset in Minion by RefineCatch Limited, Bungay, Suffolk
Printed and bound in Great Britain by MPG Books Ltd, Bodmin, Cornwall

Contents

Acknowledgements

I would like to acknowledge the help, co-operation and support of a large number of people in carrying out the work for this book. Most obviously, I would like to thank everyone who gave their time to talk to me: domestic workers, employers, employment agencies, language schools and support groups. I would also like to thank Mrs Moira Young, Head of Year 8 at Hampstead School, for helping me to locate some of my initial interviewees.

A number of academic colleagues have helped and encouraged me and given me copious amounts of their time to discuss ideas. Professor Janet Momsen first talked to me about domestic workers and has remained a source of help and support ever since. Professor Rebecca Stott suggested the idea for this book and was extremely helpful in its early stages. Dr Bridget Anderson has been an invaluable colleague, always happy to talk about domestic workers and always full of stimulating ideas. Much of the research used in this book was made possible by the Nuffield Foundation, Social Science Small Grant number SGS/00466/C. This grant made possible the employment of Rekha Narula to assist with research. Her hard work, sensitivity and enthusiasm were a great addition.

Two au pairs who were interviewed by Rekha must be particularly thanked for suggesting the title of Chapter 6, 'A life between slavery and luxury'. They said they would one day write a book with this title as it described their experiences of au pairing. I thought the phrase too good to pass over but very much hope that they will still write their book.

Preface: why domestic workers?

My interest in domestic workers developed entirely by accident when I was visiting a friend in Brazil during one Summer vacation while I was at university. I was staying in her flat in Rio de Janeiro and noticed a small room with a bathroom leading off it, on the far side of the kitchen, away from the rest of the flat. The room was unused and it was a complete mystery to me; I could not work out what it was for or what it was meant to be. It had a small bed in it but did not look like a bedroom, the walls were tiled and there was only a small, high-up window. And it was the only room in the flat to have an en suite bathroom, but the bathroom was shabby and only had cold water. In my world en suite bathrooms were a luxury of 'master bedrooms' and very unusual. I was stumped: nothing in my experience of British housing could explain to me what the room was for. Then one day my friend referred to the room as the 'maid's room' and I asked her what she meant. She explained that almost all apartments were built with a room like this, off the kitchen, away from the rest of the family, where the live-in maid was meant to live. It was taken for granted that families who could afford permanent, well-built housing would have a live-in domestic worker. I looked out of the apartment window at all the blocks across the city and thought of all the maids stacked up, one on top of another, in their little tiled boxes. There would be thousands of them, tens or hundreds of thousands, just in Rio.

In Britain I'd known a few people who had cleaners, and thought this made them very posh. I'd never known anyone with a full-time domestic worker. I had a vague notion that the royal family and other very wealthy people must have servants but I had assumed that paid domestic work had died out long ago, perhaps with corsets and coal fires. My interest in domestic workers simmered away for another few years until, encouraged by Professor Janet Momsen, I discovered there were academics studying domestic workers in Latin America. I still assumed, however, that Britain had no equivalent sector. Eventually I decided that the topic for my Ph.D.

thesis would be to discover why domestic employment was so widespread in a country like Brazil and so rare in Britain. I began to read about domestic workers in earnest. Soon after I started, in 1994 a book by Nicky Gregson and Michelle Lowe entitled *Servicing the Middle Classes: Class, Gender and Waged Domestic Labour in Contemporary Britain* was published. The authors argued that domestic employment in fact had been growing in Britain throughout the 1990s and that by their rough measure one in three dual-career, professional households employed some form of help. Their figures also suggested that this might have been a blip in the 1980s; and their work said nothing about other types of families. I decided to abandon any work on Brazil and to focus on discovering what was happening to domestic employment in Britain.

This book is based on a combination of my own primary research in London, the work of other academics studying and working with domestic workers in Britain and around the world, and a small amount of existing secondary data. Official sources are of little use in trying to find out about domestic workers. Only a small number of domestic workers appear in official measures of employment such as the census, and they do so because they are employed in the formal sector and have no other job. Other domestic workers, who work 'off the books', often have another job for more money or hours which they see as their main occupation. Alternatively, they may have a migration status that does not allow them to work legally, and thus are unlikely to declare their domestic work in any official document. This means we have to rely on proxy measures and estimates. Surveys of spending habits reveal the amounts that people spend on help in their homes and there are some figures collected on visas issued to au pairs and some other domestic workers, but there are no reliable overall figures at all.

My research has involved interviewing domestic workers, employers and agencies that place workers, and talking to groups that offer support to workers from abroad. I began interviewing agencies that placed 'top end' formal staff – such as butlers and housekeepers – in 1995, and discovered a whole world I never knew existed. In this alternative universe, staff were called by their last names, butlers ironed newspapers and housekeepers drove ahead of their employers to country houses every weekend to get things ready for their arrival. I then began interviewing agencies that place the more numerous domestic workers, nannies, mothers' helps and au pairs and I started to interview domestic workers and employers. These interviewees included cleaners, nannies and au pairs, and employers who used those types of help. In 2000, with the invaluable help of my research assistant, I surveyed au pairs attending English language classes around London and held discussions with groups of au pairs in their classes. Additionally I interviewed some as individuals. Everyone who was interviewed was assured of their confidentiality and pseudonyms have been used throughout this book. While doing this research I became increasingly aware of the precarious and undervalued place of au pairs, who have been largely ignored in debates about domestic workers. As a result, their experiences and their stories dominate some sections of the later chapters.

Filippa

On a sunny day in late October I met Filippa, an 18-year-old au pair from Sweden, working in a wealthy suburb of North London. We met at the flat where she lived and worked. It was in a large red-brick house on a quiet tree-lined road and exuded a sense of comfortable but not showy prosperity.

Filippa showed me in to the large open-plan living room, then quickly ushered me to her own room. It was just two metres square and had been made from the half landing of a staircase that was no longer used. There was a single bed, a small chest of drawers and a small television. Sitting on her narrow bed, Filippa told me about her life as an au pair in London.

Filippa had decided to become an au pair in order to improve her English and as a break between high school and university. She had dreamt of coming to London, as so many teenagers do. Au pairing seemed the perfect way to make her dream come true. She would be able to study English, to earn a bit of money, and to be part of a caring family. And, as she liked children, childcare seemed an attractive job. So, she subscribed to an au pair placement magazine, found a job with a host family and set off for London full of enthusiasm.

Her main job as an au pair was to look after a one-year-old boy. She cared for him on her own each morning and then did housework in the afternoons when his mother had finished work. Filippa liked the little boy, liked looking after him, and she did not find the housework too arduous. By the time I met her, however, Filippa was desperately unhappy.

Filippa was isolated and lonely. Her daily routine made it impossible for her to attend English classes. Her English was hardly improving and she met very few people. As the child could not yet talk, her English was rarely practised at home either. Her host family were quiet people who were not deliberately unkind but they did not include Filippa in their lives. She spent most of the day without adult company, ate all her meals alone, and passed most evenings on her own in her room. When the occasion permitted, she would visit one of the small number of au pairs whom she knew locally but she was not allowed to bring friends to the house even if the family were out. Quietly, Filippa confided to me that she was thinking of not returning to London after visiting her parents at Christmas. She said, 'I think, to be an au pair, for a few months is good, if you meet lots of people. But now, I don't know. I think it is not good to be so much alone.'

1 | What is the servant problem?

There are perhaps two million domestic workers in Britain today – more than there were in Victorian times – and 2.7 million British households now employ some kind of domestic help.[1] As well as the traditional butlers, maids, valets and cooks who wait on the super-rich, Britain is now served by tens of thousands of nannies, cleaners and au pairs as well as housekeepers, gardeners, drivers and the new domestic helpers – 'concierge services' – all ensuring the middle class live more comfortably. Global inequalities in income and opportunity provide British families with access to a cheap and plentiful supply of cleaners and childcarers, dog-walkers and gardeners. Modern society and modern domestic appliances have not, it seems, put an end to drudgery. Rather, the twenty-first century marks a new high point of domestic employment.

Why is domestic employment a problem?

In earlier times the servant problem was always thought of as the shortage of hardworking or pliable servants. Today's servant problem is different: it is that domestic employment exists and is growing. This isn't just a problem because it seems to be a throw-back to earlier, less enlightened times: it is a problem because the growth in domestic employment results from a combination of unwelcome trends. If we look at these trends that underpin the growth of the domestic labour sector, we find gender inequalities, income inequalities, racism, work practices that have become less rather than more family-friendly, and childcare provision that still basically expects women to stay at home and look after the kids.

These trends combine to make domestic employment easier, more necessary and cheaper than it might otherwise be, but equally, all of them intensify inequalities that make life worse for millions of people in Britain and elsewhere. Employing domestic help is at best an individual solution to a social problem. At worst is the use of another human being to enhance and display wealth and status. Neither is to be encouraged. The inequalities and practices that support the growth of domestic employment should be challenged and the realities of domestic work in Britain today need to be exposed.

Domestic work in a global economy

To understand the emergence of this new servant problem we need to look first at the organization of the global economy. The development of an integrated global economy and the spread of neo-liberalism have supported the growth of domestic employment in various ways. In the first place, there is now a supply of workers available for British families at relatively low cost. Secondly, inequalities within Britain have increased, creating both a supply of and demand for domestic help. Last, working conditions in Britain have been 'Americanized', leaving families with less time to carry out their own childcare and housework.

Large numbers of domestic workers come to Britain from impoverished countries in the global South or from other parts of Europe. Countries such as the Philippines and Sri Lanka have become labour exporters in order to earn foreign currency to repay their national debt. Women from these countries are encouraged by their governments to travel abroad to become domestic workers, leaving their own children while they care for the families of richer women in the north. It is estimated that money sent home by domestic workers living abroad is worth more to Asian countries than foreign aid. For Sri Lanka remittances from domestic workers are the largest source of foreign exchange.[2]

The structure of the global economy also underpins inequalities closer to home. Successive British governments have favoured policies that make businesses more 'competitive' on the global stage. These policies often mean reducing workers' rights and holding wages down. Working hours have become longer and more flexible for most groups and income inequalities have grown substantially since 1979. Changes in taxation and benefits have favoured the most wealthy and punished the worst off, driving some people to work in the informal economy as cleaners, while others are easily able to purchase substantial amounts of domestic help.

Working hours for all groups have been extended and are now more likely to include weekends and evenings. For some the result of this hard work is high earnings, perhaps augmented by big bonuses, which allows them to pay other people to cater to their needs. For others – the majority of workers – a long-hours culture does not result in high pay: it is a way to make ends meet on meagre hourly wages. For increasing numbers of people working long hours equates with taking second and even third jobs, some of them serving the 'cash rich, time poor' winners of the system.

Parents have been particularly hard hit by this new work culture. For all the government rhetoric about 'work–life balance', work seems to dominate our lives more than ever before. Childcare, however, has not changed enough to meet the needs of most working families. As working hours have increased and more women with small children go out to work, there has not been a concomitant expansion in inexpensive and easily available child-care. There has been a growth in childcare provision, but much of this has been in the form of private nurseries, which charge more than many women earn. They are only a solution for the few. The government has promoted work as the way out of poverty for everyone but so far childcare places are still rare, expensive, inaccessible and inflexible. For those with the means to pay, this makes private solutions increasingly attractive – hiring a nanny or au pair may be the cheapest way to secure childcare for the hours needed. For families who do not earn enough to pay the high costs of care, the lack of subsidized childcare places means that fewer women work or that they seek work they can organize around their children – like cleaning.

Gender inequalities – no change on the home front

In addition to the economic inequalities that result from neo-liberalism, domestic employment is supported by the gender inequalities within families. Despite the gains that women have won in the workplace and the wider public sphere they have gained almost no ground at home: women still do the vast majority of all housework and childcare regardless of whether they work part time or full time. Women even do the majority of housework in households where they work but their partners are unemployed.[3] For women who go out to work but still feel that the housework is and should be their responsibility, the amount of work they face can be a good reason to get a cleaner, particularly if they feel they can pay the cleaner with their own wages.

In families where women find that they end up doing all the housework but they want their partners to do more, employing a cleaner can be a way of stopping the arguments about whose turn it is to do chores. Some women insist that if the men they live with aren't doing their fair share they should pay the cleaner's wages. For these families the arguments have stopped and the cleaning gets done but no progress has been made: the men involved have not taken responsibility for their own share of the mess created, the work has just been passed to another, poorer, woman. Add-itionally, children who grow up in houses that have cleaners may also inherit their parents' attitudes. They fail to see cleaning as something that is done by all family members and do not learn to take responsibility for their own mess. They can grow up not knowing how to do housework and thinking of themselves as 'the type of people' who should not do their own domestic work.

Women's overwhelming responsibility for housework and childcare is also a reason why they become paid domestic workers themselves. Domestic work can 'fit' for women, both practically and psychologically. Cleaning work can be arranged around childcare for women with children at school and women find it easy to get this work because employers assume that all women know how to do it. Women also find it easier than men to get childcare jobs. Women can be steered towards this type of work from a young age and may be recommended to train in nursery nursing by teachers or careers advisors. They then find it easy to access work as nannies. Men who want to work with young children face greater difficulties. A recent survey by Mori found that 34 per cent of parents would not want their children cared for by a man and 56 per cent would be suspicious of a man who worked in childcare.[4] So domestic work remains between women – either done for free by women for their own families, or done for pay for others.

There is also a more insidious side to the long-standing assumption that domestic work is women's work: the low status that attaches to all domestic labour and the poor pay and treatment of domestic workers that goes with it. Today's domestic workers have to shoulder the centuries-long prejudices against domestic labour. These attitudes assumed that all domestic work was unskilled, that it was easy to do and that, somehow, all women were naturally able to do it. Domestic labour has been seen as trivial against the Herculean achievements of men in public life; and even studies of domestic life and labour have been disparaged as petty or laughable.[5] The pay and working conditions of contemporary domestic workers reflect these views and reinforce the place of domestic work as labour taken on only by those who have no other choices or no other skills. Domestic work is usually low paid, working conditions are poor and domestic workers' abilities are taken for granted rather than acknowledged or praised.

Dirt, cleaning and status

There is another aspect of the servant problem that deserves investigation and that is the relationship between dirt, cleaning and status. The status of both domestic work and domestic workers is caught up in complicated feelings about pollution and the people who deal with 'polluted' matter. These feelings transfer to domestic workers and affect their relationships with employers and then influence the ways domestic workers are treated. The low status of housework can be a reason people employ help at home, and the desire to banish dirt from their homes can be caught up subconsciously in people's ideas about their own status and worth.

The complexity and irrationality of our attitudes towards dirt comes out in the treatment and social status of the people who deal with dirt for a living. Despite the importance of the work to our health and general environment, work with sewage, collecting rubbish or cleaning is avoided and the people who do this work are looked down upon, assumed to be dirty themselves. The status of the worker becomes inseparable from the status of the work and it is impossible to improve dramatically the standing of either without challenging deep-seated feelings about dirt. Were everyone to do their own cleaning no one would be demeaned by this contact with dirt but, when people pay others to do cleaning for them, they create jobs and roles for others which are defined by their closeness to dirt.

While being actively involved in cleaning dirt can mean a low status for the worker who does it, having a clean home can be an indicator of high status for the owner of that house, particularly if the effort of maintaining high standards of cleanliness is invisible. Historically, having a clean house and visibly clean and well-kept clothing and household linen was a mark of high status because a clean habitat was so difficult to achieve. Cleanliness demonstrated how many servants were employed and how well those servants worked. The use of open fires, the difficulties of heating water and the lack of modern cleaning products such as soap or washing powder all meant that houses were dirtier than is the case today and that cleaning was more time-consuming and difficult. Poor people could not maintain their houses or linen to the same standards as people who had servants to work for them, so cleanliness was a sign of wealth and status. Today, a beautifully presented house can also demonstrate status, particularly if it is large or decorated in a way that is time-consuming to keep clean. Many wealthy families employ large amounts of domestic help to keep their houses pristine. A beautifully kept house displays the owner's taste and care and hints at a more leisurely life than a house where toys are left lying around or there is washing up sitting in the sink. To preserve the aura of leisured ease it is necessary not only that no dirt is ever seen but also that no cleaning is ever evident: the house implies that the owners simply are not dirty. Domestic workers in such houses have to perform their work while being imperceptible. Their work is only right if its very existence is denied.

George Bernard Shaw is reported to have said: 'When domestic servants are treated as human beings it is not worthwhile to keep them.'[6] While I perhaps wouldn't put it quite in those terms, his point is perceptive and as relevant to domestic employment today as it was when he was alive. If employers were to treat domestic workers as equal, if they made sure they didn't pass all the worst jobs to their cleaners, if they paid domestic workers what their time was really worth or if they valued the work of cleaning as much as they valued a spotless house, they would not find it worthwhile to keep them. This is an awkward truth at the centre of the relationship between domestic worker and employer. At the very least it can make things uncomfortable for everyone involved, but it is more serious than that. The low status of domestic work affects the pay and conditions of all domestic workers, making them lower than average with little chance of much improvement. Some domestic workers even find that their employers' do not bother to treat them as human. Their low status in their employers' minds means they may be beaten, starved and imprisoned.

The Great British servant problem then and now

The 'servant problem' was the traditional bugbear of the British middle and upper classes, who were supposed to have discussed endlessly over dinner the difficulties of finding and retaining reliable servants. Generation after generation of employers complained that modern servants did not know their place, didn't know when they were on to a good thing, were insubordinate and lazy. Each generation thought the problem was unique to them and due to the particular liberality of the age. So William Polderoy wrote in 1886:

> In earlier years we could reckon upon a supply of modest, willing, trustworthy girls, who, for the priviledge of working in a gentleman's household, were ready to accept a reasonable sum in the way of wages. Now thanks to the pernicious diffusion of radical ideas, everything is different. Servants ask double wages if they are called upon to leave London . . . and . . . are commonly sluttish and rude.[7]

But he was wrong in his belief that the servant problem was new. Nearly 200 years earlier Daniel Defoe was so enraged by the servant problem that in 1704 he wrote a treatise titled *The Great Law of Subordination Considered, or The Insolence and Insufferable Behavior of SERVANTS in England duly enquired into*. And Jonathan Swift's satirical and hysterical spoof manual *Directions to Servants*, first published in 1745,[8] reveals the extent of his frustration with the servants he employed over many decades. In this he mockingly advises servants to use loaves of bread as candlesticks, to wipe used cutlery on the tablecloth or to wipe their shoes on the bottom of a curtain, suggesting these are all things he has seen servants do. But his

'Directions to the Waiting-Maid' perhaps reveal more about what servant life was really like. He advises:

> If you are in a great family, and my lady's woman, my lord may probably like you, although you are not half so handsome as his own lady. In this case, take care to get as much out of him as you can, and never allow him the smallest liberty, not the squeezing of your hand, unless he puts a guinea into it . . . Five guineas for handling your breast is a cheap pennyworth, although you seem to resist with all your might, but never allow him the last favour under a hundred guineas, or a settlement of twenty pounds a year for life . . . I must caution you particularly against my lord's eldest son . . . after ten thousand promises you will get nothing from him but a big belly or a clap – and probably both together.[9]

It is no wonder really that the servant problem was perennial, given the poor treatment of servants and the persistence of their working arrangements over centuries.

At the height of the Victorian and Edwardian boom, the largest group of servants was 'maids of all work', who worked alone doing everything for a family who were probably not very well off. Pay and conditions for these women were appalling. In 1914 normal working hours were from 6.30 am until 10 pm or later and pay could be £5 a year, from which female servants also had to supply their uniforms. Frank Victor Dawes comments:

> The majority of those 'in service' in Britain were employed by the middle classes, not the aristocracy. These servants were mostly children, the maids of the kitchens, the tweeny or between-maid and bootboys. They were mere chattels and slaves, whom their employers hardly ever saw, and frequently failed to recognize when they did.[10]

Eventually other jobs became available for women – in offices, factories and shops. Most women jumped at these jobs, even though some of them paid less than service and did not provide accommodation.[11] The long hours and low status of service meant that most women thought that anything was preferable. Employers were eventually left to depend on daily 'charwomen' and on the advice of publications such as *Appearances: How to keep them up on a Limited Income*[12] and *First-Aid to the Servantless*[13] published in 1913 to help people coping without servants for the first time. Horror of horrors, some employers actually had to do their own housework, as Lady Bunting wailed in 1910:

No one to cook the dinner, answer the door, attend to the children and carry out the many other requirements of an ordinary household. In many cases the mistress is absolutely incapable of taking on the duties which the servant has done and she finds herself more of a dependent than the servant . . .[14]

And there, the history books would suggest, is the end of the story. Servant employment grew during industrialization, peaked at the turn of the twentieth century and then declined as new job opportunities became available after the World Wars. Dawes' history, written in the 1970s, describes domestic service as 'gone for good',[15] and Caroline Davidson wrote in 1983: 'It is hard to conceive how ubiquitous domestic servants once were, now that they are such a thing of the past.'[16] But domestic service did not disappear entirely. Instead, its form changed, making domestic workers more difficult to find and to count in official measures. The large formal household is much rarer than it was but has by no means disappeared, and other types of domestic work are now more important. There are estimates of 100,000 nannies working in Britain, many of them enabling professional women to go out to work. There are perhaps 50–60,000 au pairs, drawn increasingly from Eastern Europe and the former Soviet Union, and there are innumerable cleaners each working for a number of households once or twice a week.

The first part of the book looks in detail at the interrelated trends underpinning the recent growth in paid domestic employment. The second part looks more closely at what domestic work is like in contemporary Britain. Chapter 2 begins by examining international trends and looks at the global context within which paid domestic work happens. It traces why people are prepared to leave their homes and travel thousands of miles to work in other people's houses and why workers go to the places that they do. It also gives an overview of British government approaches to admitting migrant domestic workers and the ways in which policies have been adapted to attract different groups of workers at different times in the post-war period. Chapter 3 looks at the social trends within Britain that have made employing domestic help easier and more attractive. This includes women's increased engagement in paid work outside the home and particularly the growing numbers of women in well-paid work. It also examines gender roles within the home and working hours for both men and women. This chapter also traces income inequalities within Britain and demonstrates the ways that such large differences between the rich and poor feed into the domestic employment sector. Chapter 4 looks at childcare provision in Britain and shows how, even with the investment made following the

National Childcare Strategy, provision of subsidized care is inadequate for most families in most places. In such a situation, employing a nanny or au pair can actually be the cheapest option rather than a luxury.

Chapter 5 then looks at domestic employment that is very certainly a luxury rather than a necessity. It traces the different types of domestic job that exist, from the very formal 'top end' of butlers and housekeepers, to the less formal employment of nannies by mothers who do not go out to work, or of cleaners used to keep up appearances. The employment of domestic workers as a luxury rather than a necessity is much more widespread than might be imagined and accounts for many tens of thousands of jobs. Chapter 6 describes the working conditions and experiences of domestic workers. It spells out the precise pay and working arrangements of cleaners, nannies and au pairs and then looks at what it is like working and living in someone else's house. Chapter 7 asks what can be done to improve domestic work. It begins by looking at changes that could be made to domestic workers' rights and to employers' behaviour. It then goes on to highlight the broader-scale social changes that would be necessary to remove the need for the employment of domestic help and argues that these changes would be desirable for domestic workers and society more generally.

2 | Caring in the new world order

The growth of globalized domestic employment

One thing that characterizes domestic employment today and that differentiates it from domestic service in the past is its globalized nature. Millions of women travel thousands of miles around the world to work in the homes of families they have never met and perhaps cannot even talk to. This new global domestic labour market is the context of paid domestic work in the UK.

Domestic employment has been increasing in many parts of the world and migrant women make up the vast majority of this new domestic workforce. The low pay, the long and unpredictable hours, mean that few workers with any choice will take on these jobs. One hundred thousand migrant women work as domestics in Singapore, and similar numbers work in Hong Kong and the Gulf States. Canada imports domestic workers from Asia, the Caribbean and Britain, as does the USA, whilst European countries often have domestic workers from former colonies, or poorer neighbours in Southern and Eastern Europe. This chapter begins by outlining briefly the tradition of domestic workers migrating from rural to urban areas and then examines the forces underpinning the current movements of domestic workers around the world. Economic policies such as 'structural adjustment' (a type of economic reform that involves cuts in spending on welfare and increased competition from foreign companies) create conditions which force women to migrate in order to support their families. Some countries have encouraged these movements in order to increase their earnings in foreign currency and they help women move abroad to domestic jobs. Receiving countries also play their part either by adjusting immigration policies to make it easier or more difficult for women of particular nationalities to enter their labour markets, or by turning a blind eye to the employment of undocumented workers.

Migration and domestic work in historical context

Paid domestic work has long been performed by migrants. While today domestic workers may be travelling across continents, historically they were more likely to be moving from rural areas to local urban centres, or perhaps to larger cities farther away. The vast majority of these servants, in the past as now, were women. Men were employed in a range of domestic roles, but in Britain a tax on male servants, introduced in 1777, made the employment of men more expensive and thus more scarce. This had a dramatic effect on domestic roles that has carried into the present day.

Historical accounts from Europe make clear that before the industrial revolution servant employment was widespread. Servants were employed in the large households of the nobility and landed gentry and by smaller farmers or urban merchants and craftsmen. In pre-industrial times household roles were not as clearly delineated as they later became: servants could work in the house, the garden, in the dairy or on the farm, and would often be involved in a combination of activities. In rural areas children could be sent to work at the local 'big house', and some of these servants were considered lucky compared to their brothers and sisters because they were assured a roof over their head and food every day. Employers in urban areas recruited servants from the surrounding countryside, as country girls were thought to make better workers. They were considered to be stronger and healthier and not to have had their 'heads turned' by city ways.[1] In some countries, notably, the USA, Britain and France, slaves were brought over much greater distances to work as household servants. In eighteenth-century Britain black servants were considered fashionable status symbols and were often given to women as presents by fathers, husbands or lovers.

Industrialization had as great an impact on the domestic worker as it did on other parts of society. The average size of the household employing servants declined considerably, creating a situation where servants were more often isolated 'maids of all work' rather than members of a staff who had opportunities to socialize and to progress within an, albeit constrained, hierarchy. The period also saw a decline in male employment within domestic service throughout Europe and North and South America. The largest households had traditionally employed many men as well as women but, as these larger households were replaced by the smaller establishments of the new urban bourgeoisie, a single maid, or maybe two, was taken on to do all tasks.

Whilst this move from very large to small households caused a decline in the number of males employed in domestic service, it created a demand for more servants overall, as many more families were able to afford a small domestic staff. As we have seen, these jobs were taken on by young women from rural areas. Theresa McBride, in her book *The Domestic Revolution*, described service as being like a holding area where young women waited until the new towns and cities could supply them with alternative opportunities. When women were able to take jobs as clerks and factory workers, the supply of servants declined and the average age of servants increased.[2] Likewise, in areas where other work existed for women, such as the mill towns of Lancashire, service was a less important form of employment.[3]

Between 1750 and 1850, in many parts of the world men withdrew from domestic employment as new opportunities opened up for them and the jobs they had traditionally held in households disappeared. In Britain this trend was helped along by the tax on the employment of male domestic servants introduced in 1777. The tax was imposed in order to raise money to fight the American War of Independence and to encourage men to join the Navy. Its effect was to remove male servants from all but the most prestigious households and to make the employment of male servants a sign of wealth. This meant that domestic and non-domestic roles became firmly divided as employers could no longer afford to let their male farm labourers or apprentices work in the house on a casual basis as they had done previously. Where men were employed as servants they were given the roles which were the most visible to guests – as footmen and butlers, for instance – so that the extravagance of their employers could not be over-looked. As the tax was not removed until 1937, a clear separation of domestic and non-domestic male and female roles was clearly established within large British houses that remains to this day. By 1851 some 89.9 per cent of indoor servants in Britain were female. By 1911 this had risen to 91.7 per cent.

During the late Victorian period, when domestic service was rapidly expanding and equally rapidly becoming dominated by women, the status of service as an occupation changed. It went from being a job which was respected and well paid, to perhaps the lowest-status work available. The originally relatively high status of the job is illustrated by the fact that in the late eighteenth century and early nineteenth century in Latin America and the Caribbean statutes existed restricting domestic work to white and mixed race women. Black and indigenous people were banned. In the United States domestic work was largely undertaken by American-born women rather than more recent migrants, and in 1870, two-thirds of all female non-agricultural wage-earners worked as domestics in private houses. In Europe service was a favoured occupation for daughters and was seen as a job with prospects. Many maids left service by marrying a lower-middle-class or skilled working man. They were thought to make good and 'respectable' wives because of what they had learnt from living alongside their 'betters'.[4]

By the end of the nineteenth century, however, the status of domestic work had changed. It had gone from being a profession of choice to a job of last resort. With this decline in status the composition of the servant population changed. Domestic work rapidly became the occupation for those without other choices. Often these people were migrants, without contacts in urban areas and members of minority ethnic groups who were excluded from more attractive work. In Latin America indigenous women from rural areas replaced white women as domestics in urban centres. In the USA recent migrants from Germany, Scandinavia and Ireland took these jobs in the north-east and midwest, later to be replaced by black women from the south. In the south-west and west at the end of the nineteenth century, domestic work was carried out by Mexican-American, Mexican, African-American and Native American women and Asian men (who worked as 'houseboys' in northern California). Later, Japanese, Mexican and Chicana women came to dominate the sector, with government-sponsored training manuals and domestic vocational training schools deliberately channelling Mexican and Chicana women into the sector until the 1970s.[5] In Europe, women and men from the local area were replaced by migrants from more distant and marginalized rural areas as well as from other countries.

Thus by the beginning of the twentieth century a situation existed where domestic service was the largest single employer of women in industrialized countries, accounting for nearly 16 per cent of the total workforce in Britain in 1891, yet it was also the most denigrated job, one which attracted migrant women with few other choices who worked long hours in isolated conditions for low pay. Opportunities for women, however, increased most strikingly during the two world wars and fewer and fewer women were prepared to enter this type of work. This had two effects: the number of servants employed fell and servants began to move over greater distances to fill the situations that local women, now with more choices, would no longer take on.

There are many accounts of a 'servant crisis' finally occurring in Britain after the Second World War. During the war, women left service to work in a wide variety of jobs and few of them were interested in returning to domestic work when the war was over. During the 1950s middle-class women who could no longer employ servants had to run homes single-handed for the first time and there are some accounts of women not being prepared to entertain at home any more as they were embarrassed by their servantless state. Slowly, however, the norms of family life changed for the lower middle class, and appliances came to replace the labour of people – for those who could afford them. Lavish dinner parties were no longer expected and homes became smaller and easier to maintain. New guide-books and magazines gave women advice on ways to reduce their workload. Brass stair rods were replaced with wooden ones that would not need polishing, silver was no longer left on display to tarnish, and paper napkins were advised as a replacement for linen. Husbands were even advised to come home early from work once a week to help turn the mangle on washdays.[6] New ways of obtaining help were found and the 'daily lady' or 'charwoman' became the effective replacement to the 'maid of all work'. Live-out dailies and chars were often older, married women, who carried out housekeeping duties such as cleaning, shopping, cooking and ironing for one or more local families. The 'daily', so called because she came in every day but lived out, has since been replaced in many middle-class households by a cleaner who visits less frequently and carries out a more limited range of duties. The au pair scheme was also developed at this time (and formalized in 1969) to give some help to middle-class housewives facing life without domestic help for the first time.

The wealthy, however, continued to live in luxury and to employ servants to support their lifestyles. The shortage of British women prepared to do this work created a demand for migrants from farther afield. Initially these women came from Ireland and domestic service was the most common occupation for Irish women in Britain until the 1950s. In fact, Irish women were in particular demand from the end of the nineteenth century because they were seen as more amenable than British women and strong enough to do heavy household work. Before then they were the least favoured servants and faced extensive prejudice, which meant they could only find jobs as general servants for lower-middle-class and working-class families.[7] Later on, women were recruited from the rest of Europe and other parts of the world to work as live-in domestics. Work permits remained available for domestic jobs even in times when other forms of migration were restricted because of the shortage of British women who were prepared to take on the work.

The twentieth century saw the decline of domestic service in many industrialized countries and the development of new forms of live-out, flexible and part-time domestic help. However, by the end of the century, domestic employment in Britain was increasing and by some measures more servants were employed in the 1990s than in the 1890s.[8]

The global labour market

Structural adjustment policies and neo-liberalism

Since the 1980s the global economic context has been one of expanding neo-liberalism, an economic philosophy that supports private enterprise, reduces state spending and encourages global competition. For many Less Developed Countries this has meant the imposition of Structural Adjustment Policies (SAPs) by agencies such as the World Bank or IMF, to whom they are indebted. SAPs are programmes of financial reform that poor countries are forced to follow in order to be considered for further loans. The SAPs are designed to cut government spending and encourage foreign investment and include measures such as reducing expenditure on health and education programmes, ending food subsidies, reducing wage rates, devaluing local currency and privatizing state-owned enterprises. These measures are meant to promote efficiency and competitiveness in the adjusting country and so create future wealth through the resultant expansion of the private sector. In practice they have worked in the interests of multinationals, who are able to access new markets and cheap labour more easily.

Grace Chang, author of *Disposable Domestics: Immigrant Workers in the Global Economy*, has reported on the way that SAPs have affected women specifically and have underpinned the migration strategies of domestic workers. In many countries throughout the developing world women have been adversely affected by SAPs. Cuts in public expenditure add to women's burdens in various ways. Reductions in health care programmes are particularly punishing to women. In the first place they mean that the care of sick and elderly family members falls to them. At the same time, women's own health suffers because of the reductions in prenatal and postnatal care. Additionally, there are charges for access to other health care services. The introduction of charges restricts women's access to health care specifically, since households with few resources often give priority to the health of men because men's work is more likely to be paid, or better paid than women's.

This comes at a time when average nutritional levels are also declining because of the abolition of food subsidies and changes in agricultural practices. This further reduces the health status of many people and undermines their ability to fight illness. Women may again be worse affected than men. As with health care, families may choose to give priority to the nutrition of the men in the household, for the same reason. Accordingly, women and girls have access to the least food or the least nutritious food. Similarly, when charges are introduced for schooling, girls are more likely to be kept home than boys, or girls may be withdrawn from school to help their mothers with additional work at home. In the long run this decline in girls' education can have profound effects; mothers with more years of schooling are more likely to have smaller families, to have higher birth-weight babies and to have children that survive the first years of life.

In rural areas the introduction of SAPs can mean the move from small-scale and subsistence agriculture to the production of cash crops for export. Cash crops do not feed local people and the intensive agriculture employed is more likely to use mechanical and chemical inputs than labour to increase yields. The result is that there is less work and less food available as well as damage to the environment. As a consequence of these changes women have entered the formal and informal workforce in greater numbers. Male earnings have fallen and male unemployment has grown. At the same time new world-market factories have targeted women for their 'nimble fingers' and docile demeanours.

In some circumstances, however, these 'invisible adjustments' by women are not enough to provide for their children and other dependants. They may have no option but to go farther afield in search of work. For some women these moves will be from their rural homes to local cities but for many others the journey will be over thousands of miles. It is often the better educated who end up travelling the farthest. This is because they are more likely to be able to afford the upfront costs of agency fees and airfares, and also because they have skills that are in demand elsewhere.

Many of those migrating have specific technical skills – such as nurses, doctors or engineers – or they have the language skills that help them find domestic work abroad. This supply of skilled and well-educated labour exists because of the cut-backs in public spending resulting from the imposition of SAPs. In some countries jobs for public sector workers have been cut, in others wages no longer cover the costs of the most basic necessities, and in some countries jobs exist but wages are not paid for months at a time. In these circumstances some of the most valuable and highly trained people leave their home countries and families to take on unskilled work caring for the families of the better-off in richer countries. It is not uncommon to find qualified teachers or university-educated professionals travelling to the Middle East, North America or Europe to work as domestics.

As well as the economic effects of neo-liberal globalization, violence or the threat of violence can underpin the decision to migrate in search of domestic work. Bridget Anderson[9] has explored the migration strategies of domestic workers in six European countries and discovered that many of them were escaping violent situations. The violence may have come from husbands or other family members, or could be the result of political upheavals and civil war. Anderson found that domestic workers from South

America, Asia and Africa cited the poor political and economic conditions in their home countries as reasons for migration. Some were specifically at risk if they did not leave, as an Ethiopian woman working in Athens explained:

> I came in 1988. Mengistu was in power then. You were forced to be a member of the party. Unless you were a member of the party you couldn't work or talk. I was told I would be fined and jailed unless I joined the party so I was running around bribing and fixing my pass-port to get out – very fast. My father was imprisoned and my brother was killed ... at the time I just wanted to save my life ... I had a tourist visa for 15 days. The UN would not accept my claim. I cannot leave. I work as a domestic.[10]

Other women were escaping forced or violent marriages and for some of these migration abroad was the only option. Anderson cites the example of Morocco, where women who leave their husbands can be reported to the police who can pursue them within the national boundaries. Escape to another country is the only way to avoid being returned to their husbands or imprisoned.

Domestic workers can also be victims of trafficking into Europe, often as children, or can be sold to employers by their parents and then taken abroad. Gaby Hinsliff reports that every year as many as 10,000 children from West Africa enter the UK through private fostering arrangements and a significant percentage of these are destined to work as domestics without pay. Their parents agree to the arrangements because they believe their children will be educated in Britain.[11] Children can also be sent to work as domestics in local urban centres and end up being taken abroad by employ-ers. In these circumstances children are particularly vulnerable: they lose contact with their parents and are denied an education as well as living in harsh conditions, often without sufficient food and sleep. Children as young as 8 or 9 years old can be employed to care for younger children, to clean and to cook meals.[12]

Labour export

The journeys that domestic workers make are not only the result of indi-vidual choices or household survival strategies. Certain countries, most notably the Philippines and Sri Lanka, have developed government policies to export labour as a way of earning foreign currency to repay debts and to ease the effects of mass unemployment. These countries see their populations as a resource that can be exported and they actively encourage and assist the migration of nationals to work abroad. Some highly skilled workers, such as doctors, may be able to get equivalent posts in other countries, but other workers are encouraged to take whatever work they can. Men work in construction and other heavy manual work and women take jobs as domestics. As President Marcos of the Philippines said in 1982:

> For us, overseas employment addresses two major problems: unemployment and the balance of payments position. If these problems are met or at least partially so by contract migration, we also expect an increase in national savings and investment levels.[13]

Remittances – the money sent home by workers from abroad – now account for more than 10 per cent of the Philippines' GNP and huge numbers of Filipino doctors and an even larger proportion of registered nurses now work outside the Philippines. In 1993 alone, 21,000 medical professionals left the country.[14] The policy of labour export started by President Marcos was accelerated under President Aquino when IMF-imposed import liberalization policies made imports more expensive and the Philippine peso weaker. Between 1986 and 1989 637,000 migrants left the Philippines as contract workers each year. By the early 1990s about 3.5 million Filipinos were working in 120 different countries around the world.[15]

Sri Lanka became a major exporter of labour after 1977 when government liberalization policies caused an increase in poverty, a fall in real wages and an increase in imports. The government enthusiastically embraced labour export as a solution to the ensuing problems and facilitated the migration of skilled and unskilled workers by establishing missions abroad, subsidizing migrants' airfares and even giving government employees the right to two years' leave in order to work abroad.[16]

Both the Philippines and Sri Lanka have government agencies to organize and facilitate the export of labour. Sri Lanka established the Bureau of Foreign Employment (BFE) in 1985 to monitor recruitment agencies, to promote employment opportunities overseas and to protect migrants. It also works directly as an employment service, linking migrants to jobs abroad. The Philippines established the Philippine Overseas Employment Administration (POEA) in 1982 to deal with all areas of labour migration. It has a role in marketing and advertising Filipino labour abroad as well as licensing employment agencies and acting as an agency itself.

Despite this government involvement, most migrant workers still use agencies in the private sector that can behave in the most unscrupulous ways. Even those who do use government agencies, or licensed agencies, are

not protected from corruption. Domestic workers from developing countries pay recruitment fees to agencies to find them work in the Middle East,
Hong Kong, Singapore and elsewhere. They then have to repay fees and
airfares from their earnings with interest. Even the fees charged by govern-
ment-licensed agencies can be high, the equivalent of more than a year's
income, and if charged up front, domestic workers often have to sell land or
possessions or borrow money to pay them. As well as their fees agencies can
charge for an airfare that has already been paid by an employer. On arrival
at her new job a domestic worker can find herself repaying a debt to an
agent and having deductions made from her wages by employers to cover
what they have paid out. Some domestic workers are offered fictitious jobs
and then dumped in faraway places or they are told that the job they were
offered has been filled but their debt still exists and they must work as
prostitutes to repay the agency.[17]

Domestic labour attracts migrants for a number of reasons. Live-in paid
domestic work provides housing as well as a job and can save a new migrant
from having to find somewhere to live in a new, strange place. The live-in
nature also allows this work to mimic certain elements of familial relationships and exploits the myth that the home is a safe space for women. Thus
women may be found entering this form of work at a younger age than
would be the case for other types of work. In addition, the near-universal
expectation that all women know how to do domestic labour and childcare
means that domestic workers rarely have to prove their abilities or show
qualifications, except at the highest levels. Therefore, there are lower barriers to entry, particularly for those moving internationally, than would be
the case with many other forms of work.

Who goes where?

The movements of domestic workers around the world are not random.
There is a pronounced pattern of movement from and to particular places
that reflects historical and colonial relationships, economic inequalities
and language commonalities. The numerous studies of migrant domestic
workers that have emerged in the last 15 years have discussed the precise
patterns of migration and have revealed a situation in which women from
particular countries, regions or even towns, migrate to specific other countries and cities. The fact that domestic workers are migrants is nothing
new but the exact patterns of migration and the scale of movements
around the world are historically contingent and may reflect centuries-old
relationships between places as well as the current political and economic
climate.

The jobs that people enter in their destination country may also be a product of their country of origin. People from particular places are assumed to be suited to particular types of domestic work or to have certain skills and characteristics. Generally, but not exclusively, women from less developed countries are most often assumed to be suited to cleaning. Women from richer countries are more likely to be involved in childcare. Even when people from different places are ostensibly carrying out the same tasks, their nationality may determine their job title and level of pay. So, for example, Filipina women working in Canada and carrying out housework and childcare are likely to be considered as 'housekeepers', while European women in the same situation are called 'nannies'. The European women are paid on average $100 a month more, even when doing the same work.[18]

Asia has been the most important source area for domestic workers for many years. There is a general pattern of richer Asian countries importing labour from their poorer neighbours and also of some countries exporting labour to other parts of the world. So, domestic workers from south and south-east Asia have moved to oil-rich countries in western Asia. It is estimated that about 160,000 move this way each year, 100,000 legally and 60,000 by more clandestine means. The largest numbers appear to be from Indonesia, Sri Lanka, the Philippines, India and Thailand. Women from these poorer Asian countries have also moved to rapidly industrializing areas such as Hong Kong, Singapore and Malaysia. Women from the Philippines, Sri Lanka and Thailand also work as domestics in North America and Europe. Often they move to these areas after working in the Gulf States, Hong Kong or Singapore.[19] Jobs in Hong Kong are even advertised in the Philippines as offering the 'golden chance to work in Canada after contract'.[20]

This movement of women from Asia has changed the composition of the domestic labour force in North America. In Canada there was a long tradition of women from the Caribbean working in domestic jobs but they have been replaced by Filipinas and some Europeans in the last 15 years. Asian women tend to considered as 'housekeepers' or housekeeper/nannies in Canada, while European women, particularly British women with an NNEB qualification, are seen as 'professional' nannies.[21] Filipinas also work as housekeepers in the United States, particularly the north-east seaboard. Women from Mexico and Central America have tended to move to the west and south-west of the USA. Estimates of the numbers of domestic workers in the United States are particularly difficult to come by because of the largely informal nature of the sector there. However, as an indication of the size of the sector and its rapid growth, we know that about two million people were employed as gardeners and domestic workers in Los Angeles according to the 1990 census. This was about twice the number recorded in 1980 and made up more than half of all the adults who had emigrated to Los Angeles since 1965.[22] Less than 1 per cent of domestic workers were American-born, the vast majority coming from Mexico, Guatemala and El Salvador.

In Latin America domestic employment is widespread, accounting for about one-fifth of all the economically active women for most countries. In general, domestic workers in Latin America tend to be internal migrants from rural areas but they may not have any more in common with their employers than domestic workers who have travelled across continents. In much of Latin America, particularly the Andean countries, rural populations are mostly made up of indigenous people who speak little Spanish. Typically employers in urban centres will identify as white, or 'mestizo/a' (mixed race) and speak Spanish.[23] Domestic workers can find themselves living with families who dress differently, eat different food, speak a different language and practise a different religion. In Brazil domestic workers also tend to be rural to urban migrants, largely from the poor north-east region. Whilst they are rarely indigenous peoples they are often ethnically different from their employers, being black or mixed race rather than white. Brazil had a long history of importing slaves from Africa and today has the second-largest population of black Africans of any country in the world; only Nigeria has more African people living in it than Brazil. The black population was originally concentrated in sugar-producing areas, which are now some of the poorest parts of the country. Black migrant women from these areas are an important part of the domestic labour force in the urban south-east. Some domestic workers do cross national boundaries to work in richer South American countries, for example, in the capital of Argentina, Buenos Aires, there are domestic workers from Chile, Paraguay and Bolivia.[24]

Within Europe there has been a general pattern of movement of women from poorer areas in the South and East to the richer areas of the North and West. Many countries also import domestic workers from places further away but with which they have historical and colonial links. Traditionally, women from Ireland and the Caribbean worked in Britain, Algerians in France, and Surinamese women worked in the Netherlands. More recently migrants from within Europe have become more important and Portuguese women have made up a large part of the domestic workforce in Britain. Polish women have been important in Germany[25] and Slovenian women in Italy.[26] Colonial history and language commonalities still have some impacts on patterns of movement. Britain gives priority to people from the Commonwealth, and France attracts domestic workers from the Overseas Departments of Martinique and Guadeloupe. Spain has large numbers of domestic workers from the Dominican Republic, the Philippines and Colombia.

Immigration policies

The move in search of domestic and other forms of low-paid care work has, as we have seen, been possible both because of the demand for workers in economically developed countries, a demand caused by the scaling back of welfare states[27] and because of the relative wealth of the middle class in the global North. The spread of neo-liberalism has meant cuts in health, welfare and education programmes throughout the world, not only in less developed nations. In some circumstances pay and working conditions in parts of the public sector have deteriorated to such an extent that recruitment of staff becomes difficult.[28] In Britain this has been seen dramatically in the health service, where shortages of doctors, nurses and other specialists have made headline news. One solution adopted by first world governments to address these staff shortages is to import labour from other parts of the world, including less developed countries. New visa schemes and recruitment agencies have been established to draw qualified workers to Britain to fill posts that cannot be filled more locally. Despite government guidelines that are supposed to prohibit the recruitment of staff from the poorest countries that desperately need skilled health care professionals themselves, the movement of these workers goes on. In 2001 about 40 per cent of new entrants to nursing in the UK were recruited from abroad and the countries supplying the largest numbers of nurses were the Philippines, South Africa, Australia, India and Zimbabwe.[29] In 2000 health and associated professionals formed the largest group of work permit holders in Britain and about 26 per cent of doctors currently working in the National Health Service were trained overseas. The most important source countries for doctors included India, Pakistan and Nigeria.[30]

Another effect of neo-liberal cuts in welfare spending is that, with the provision of services having been reduced, responsibility has been reallocated to 'the community' – often meaning the family and, specifically, women. This has been the case with much elder care, convalescent care for the sick and frail, or care for people with disabilities (see Chapter 3). The transfer of responsibilities to individual households has fed the demand for domestic workers in private homes. This demand, however, is not simply created by a lack of provision in the public sphere but by a combination of changing gender roles, work experiences, lifestyle choices and ambitions (see Chapter 3). These changing expectations and experiences create a demand for services that are not met in the public sector or elsewhere. So, for example, as women have entered the paid workforce in larger numbers, there has been neither a change in male attitudes towards carrying out housework nor the provision of adequate childcare facilities by local authorities.

The workers filling the gaps in public and private needs have much in common. They are often from the same places, may be members of the same families and may even be the same people working double shifts or moving between jobs. They are likely to face the same low pay and poor conditions and to be subject to punishing and exclusionary migration regimes. While the governments of economically developed countries may have been quick to depend on migrant workers to fill the gaps in the labour force, they have been considerably slower to recognize the contribution of domestic workers and to extend full citizenship rights to them. Domestic workers have often found it particularly difficult to be recognized as 'real' workers and 'real' migrants with the concomitant rights.

A number of countries have developed specific schemes for importing migrant domestic labour. These schemes tend to depend on domestic workers living in their employers' homes. The schemes may not give domestic workers the same protection against low pay and long hours as other workers and, often, neither do they allow domestic workers to migrate permanently or to bring their children or partners to live with them.

One of the strictest schemes of this kind is operated in Hong Kong, which had over 160,000 foreign domestic workers in 1996.[31] Here, migrant domestic workers are recruited on two-year contracts that stipulate job rules, task timetables and appearance. Domestic workers can find they are banned from having long hair or wearing make-up and must submit to compulsory pregnancy tests as part of their visa regulations. Nicole Constable found that it was not uncommon for employers in Hong Kong to issue lists of instructions to domestic workers that tried to control every area of their life and sometimes directly contradicted official employment contracts. One such list that she quoted included the following instructions to the domestic worker:

- A maid must always be polite and greet the employer, his family GOOD MORNING, GOOD DAY, GOOD AFTERNOON, GOOD EVENING OR GOOD NIGHT (before going to bed), SIR, MADAM, etc. Don't forget to say THANK YOU at appropriate times.
- *DO NOT* use any nail polish on finger and toes. *DO NOT* put on make up, even when you are going out to do the family shopping.

Your hair must be short and tidy. *DO NOT* wear tight jeans and pants and low-cut T-shirts while you are working. *DO NOT* go to the parlour in pyjamas.
- Must take bath daily before going to bed. Hand wash your own clothes separately from those of your employers and the children (especially underwear), unless your employer allows you to wash your clothes by the washing machine together with theirs.[32]

A similar scheme for importing migrant domestic labour is operated in Singapore, which employs about 100,000 foreign domestic workers – one for every eight families in the city. Domestic workers are recruited directly from their home countries through agencies and sign a two-year contract. During this time they may not leave the country without a release paper from their employer and are entitled to only one day off a month. In addition they have to sign a statement prohibiting them from marrying or cohabiting with a Singaporean citizen or permanent resident and have to take a pregnancy test every six months. Domestic workers' passports are regularly held by their employers who are also allowed to retain 20 per cent of a worker's earnings to cover the costs of their return passage. While employers are allowed to replace domestic workers within this period, a domestic worker voluntarily leaving an employer must return home and, if insufficient notice is given, must forfeit a portion of her salary.[33]

It is not only the city-states of Asia that have pursued this method of recruiting migrant domestic workers while denying them the rights of other employees. Canada operates the 'live-in caregiver programme' as a way of meeting demands for child and elder care. The programme allows workers into Canada for a period of two years with the condition that they have a contract for employment as a caregiver in a family and will live in with that family. After two years workers are allowed to apply for an open visa and later for 'landed-migrant status' – the Canadian equivalent to the US 'green card'. The programme treats domestic workers differently from other migrant workers by considering them as temporary visitors for the first two years, rather than allowing them to become landed migrants on arrival.[34] The additional stipulation that they live in makes them vulnerable to abuse and overwork, and they are also exempt from many of the employment protections that cover other workers. As Abigail Bakan and Daiva Stasiulis put it in their book *Not One of the Family: Foreign Domestic Workers in Canada*:

'Canada shares with more authoritarian regimes a glaring willingness and indeed determination to exploit female migrant domestic workers from developing countries whose limited wage earning options have made them particularly vulnerable to political and legal control.'[35]

In contrast to these specifically developed schemes the United States does not have a formal government policy or system to recruit migrant domestic workers. Employers can 'sponsor' a migrant for their green card by documenting that a US citizen is not available to do a particular job. This method has been used to bring domestic workers to the USA to work for particular families. However, writers have commented that the method more often used to bring domestic workers from abroad is the 'blind eye' turned by immigration authorities.[36] The Immigration and Naturalization Service has traditionally served employers by ignoring the employment of undocumented migrants in private homes and some employers deliberately seek out undocumented domestic workers because they will accept lower wages and will be less likely to insist on their employment rights. Doreen Mattingly has found in her research that legislation designed to reduce illegal immigration from Mexico to the USA has actually fuelled the growth in the employment of undocumented migrants as domestic workers. The Immigration Reform and Control Act (IRCA), passed in 1986, made it illegal for employers to hire undocumented workers. Before this it was illegal for such workers to seek work but their employers had not committed an offence by employing them. The Act made it much more difficult for undocumented migrants to work in the USA and a larger proportion of them sought work that was informal and hidden from the immigration authorities, as domestic work is. In addition, the Act had the effect of driving down work opportunities and conditions for all migrants, even those who were legal, as many employers would no longer hire them. This had the knock-on effect of reducing the incomes of migrant households that had been dependent on a male wage earner and of pushing more migrant women into work to make up the loss in earnings. Mattingly comments that, because of the efficiency with which it has driven migrant women into domestic labour as nannies and housekeepers, 'The IRCA may well be the country's most effective policy for supporting professional women.'[37]

The extent of the informal employment of domestic workers in the USA was brought out in the 'Zoë Baird incident'. When newly elected as president of the United States, Bill Clinton selected first Kimba Wood and then Zoë Baird as nominees for the post of Attorney General. In a series of events that was both shocking and comical each of the two women was revealed to be unappointable because they were employing undocumented domestic labour and not paying the correct employment taxes or social security payments. Much of the press coverage that followed the incident revealed an acceptance of the employment of undocumented migrants by middle-class Americans. This included a piece in the *New York Times* by Erica Jong which argued that women's groups should defend Baird and Wood and that 'We should be marching down Fifth Avenue waving banners that say "I hired an illegal alien" '. In such pieces employing women were clearly portrayed as the oppressed group and the employment or immigration rights of their employees were not considered. The fact that Baird's household income at the time was US$600,000 a year and she could easily afford to pay the wages of a documented worker and any ensuing taxes was lost on such commentators.[38] According to Pierrette Hondagneu-Sotelo, a professor at the University of Southern California, one outcome of the widespread informalization of domestic work in the USA is to reinforce the idea that it is not a real job but rather is a private arrangement beyond the notice of government or other regulating agencies.

Migration and domestic work in Britain

While Britain does not have a specific scheme to aid the migration of paid domestic workers, as Canada has, it does have a range of immigration schemes that allow people to enter the country to take on domestic work. In common with other countries, migrant domestic workers in Britain tend to have fewer rights than other migrant workers and to be less protected by law. In addition, many domestic workers are employed informally, or are undocumented, reducing their security still further. Britain is currently suffering from a pronounced shortage of low-skilled workers but is able to attract a global workforce in part because of the role of English as a global language, an incidental outcome of the increasingly global labour market. Many prospective migrants speak English or want to learn it in order to increase their employability at home or in North America. People come to Britain from all around the world to work as domestics. They may be brought by their employers, have entered on work permits, when these were available, be undocumented, be from the European Economic Area (EEA) countries (and thus be allowed to work freely in Britain), or be in the au pair scheme. Each of these avenues brings domestic workers into British homes.

Until 1975 work permits were issued to women wishing to enter Britain to work as 'domestics' in hotels, hospitals, nursing homes or private houses. In 1975 the situation changed and work permits for women were restricted to 'skilled' workers. Resident domestic workers were specifically excluded from the restrictions and a quota for their numbers was set. This allowed a limited number of women to enter Britain each year to work as domestics.

In 1975 some 66 per cent of these women came from the Philippines. From August 1977 only European women were allowed to fill quota places and at the end of 1979 the quota was phased out entirely.[39] Women from some European countries continued to move to the UK to work in the domestic sector when EU rules allowed free movement between countries and gave all EU nationals the right to work anywhere in the Union. Domestic jobs remained attractive because networks of friends and family members had been established, jobs could be found easily and women from some countries, most notably Spain and Portugal, had reputations as good domestic workers, which meant they could find better jobs and higher pay in Britain.

Another route to Britain for migrant domestic workers has been with their employers. This was allowed through a 'concession' in the immigration rules that existed until 1998. The concession allowed domestic workers to enter the UK with their employers if they had worked for that employer for at least 12 months abroad, if they would be provided with accommodation by them in the UK, and if they would remain in their employment for the duration of their stay in Britain. In other words, wealthy families coming to Britain from abroad were allowed to bring their domestic workers with them and those workers had to stay in their employment once they were here or leave the country. The visas granted to these domestic workers would depend on the visa of their employer. Those entering with employers on a visitor's visa would also be given a visitor's visa even though they were working; others would have a named employer recorded on their visas. Still others would be considered 'family members' and given no visa independent of their employer at all.

The concession was introduced because it was thought that business people would not come to Britain if they could not bring their servants. As Lord Reay put it in a House of Lords debate on domestic workers:

> Looking at our national interest, if wealthy investors, skilled workers and others with the potential to benefit our economy were unable to be accompanied by their domestic staff they might not come here at all but take their money and skills to other countries only too keen to welcome them.[40]

The effect of the concession was effectively to enslave those domestic workers who entered with their employers. As these domestic workers were not allowed to remain in Britain if they left their employer they were vulnerable to every type of abuse. Few had the resources to return to their home countries and many employers retained their employees' passports and withheld wages whilst they were in Britain. The domestic workers then had the choice of staying with their employers or leaving them and becoming undocumented workers in Britain. If they took this option they not only risked detection by immigration authorities, and thus deportation, they were also vulnerable to new employers who knew they were undocumented and could threaten them with being reported.

In the Summer of 1984 the staff at the Commission for Filipino Migrant Workers (CFMW) in London started to notice that they were increasingly being contacted by women who had become undocumented after leaving abusive employers who had brought them to Britain. Bridget Anderson has recorded the experiences of these workers, who told stories of the most horrific abuse as well as routine maltreatment, the withholding of pay and long hours without breaks. By the 1990s about 200 workers a year were contacting Kalayaan, a group established by the CFMW to support migrant domestic workers. Of 1,000 cases recorded by Kalayaan of domestic workers seeking help after leaving their employers 87 per cent reported psychological abuse, 40 per cent physical abuse, 12 per cent sexual abuse, 39 per cent were locked in by employers, 56 per cent did not have their own bed, 38 per cent had no regular food, 90 per cent were denied time off and the average length of a working day was 17.7 hours. Such figures revealed that there were not just a few bad employers mistreating a few domestic workers but rather that the immigration status of these workers made them extremely vulnerable to all forms of maltreatment.[41]

After a long campaign by domestic workers and their supporters the law was changed in 1998. Domestic workers can no longer be brought to Britain by their employers so easily and once here they are able to change employers if they are victims of abuse. The change in the law has also meant that those domestic workers who became undocumented because they had left abusive employers would be offered the chance to regularize their immigration status and stay in Britain. Whilst the concession no longer exists it has had an impact on the number of migrant domestic workers in the country. Those domestic workers who escape abusive employers tend to stay in domestic employment because it is informal, provides accommodation as well as work and is hidden from detection by immigration authorities. Some workers who have been able to regularize their immigration status have stayed in domestic positions as well.[42]

Au pairs

One of the most often overlooked ways that migrant domestic workers are recruited to Britain is through the au pair scheme. The scheme has become increasingly important and was extended in 2003 to include more countries in Eastern Europe and the former Soviet Union. While figures for the total number of au pairs are difficult to come by the government recorded

12,000 au pairs entering the country from outside the European Economic Area in 2000, and probably an equal number each year come in from European countries which do not require a visa.

The au pair scheme is an agreement between a group of European countries[43] that is meant to allow cultural exchange for young people and provide a bit of help to families with young children. Au pairs can come from any EEA member countries or a list of other European countries. Until the end of 2002 this excluded much of Eastern Europe but recently seven Eastern European countries were incorporated into the scheme because the British government was concerned that the expansion of the EU would restrict the number of au pairs available to British families.

Au pairs must be aged between 17 and 27 years, cannot be married or have dependent children. They can stay in Britain for up to two years but must leave the country within a week if they are not living with a 'host family'. Au pairs are meant to live as members of their employer's family and should be treated as equals (the translation of the phrase 'au pair') rather than as paid servants. They are meant to do 25 hours a week of 'light housework' or childcare plus two evenings of babysitting. They must have the opportunity to learn English, although employers do not have to contribute to the cost of language classes. The Home Office advises that au pairs are given £45 per week plus their own room and meals. Au pairs do not have work permits but au pair visas, and employers do not have to pay tax or national insurance for them.[44]

The au pair scheme has tended to be thought of as a cultural exchange or education programme rather than a way of importing cheap domestic help. In the past it probably did tend to attract more middle-class women from Western Europe who were taking a 'gap year' before university, or in earlier times, filling a couple of years and gaining experience of housekeeping and childcare before marriage. However, more recently the scheme has grown in size and is now an important source of live-in domestic help, particularly for families with school-age children. The scheme now includes men as well as women and highly educated graduates as well as those who have just finished at school. Au pairs often work long hours, sometimes in an arrangement called an 'au pair plus' and might not be attending English classes or improving their language skills. In other words, while some au pairs do use the scheme as a way to travel, gain experience and learn English in the protected and comfortable setting of a British family, other 'au pairs' are very low-paid, undocumented migrant workers without any rights or protection under the law, employed by families in Britain as the cheapest form of full-time, live-in domestic labour.

The extensive literature on migrant domestic workers has highlighted their vulnerability to abuse and overwork at the hands of their employers.

Au pairs have generally been excluded from these discussions as they are not thought to be as tied to their jobs. As they do not have dependent children at home, and as travelling home should be cheaper and easier for a European au pair than for a domestic worker from Sri Lanka or the Philippines, it has been assumed that au pairs are not dependent on their employers to the same extent. However, many au pairs come to Britain because they cannot find work closer to home. They hope that by studying English they will be able to improve their place in local labour markets or that they will be able to migrate more permanently. Au pairs are economic migrants, trying to find a route to a better life in the future, even if au pairing is just a step along the way. While they may not be as vulnerable as some other groups of migrant domestic workers, their migrant status, youth and their need to stay in Britain to improve their English, mean that they may still put up with poor treatment from employers and that their working conditions are often of a highly exploitative nature.

Another arrangement that is couched in similar terms of 'cultural exchange' is the Working Holidaymaker Scheme. This allows citizens of the Commonwealth and British Dependent Territories to work in Britain for up to two years. The scheme is described as 'a cultural experience for young people to sample the British way of life for an extended period. During this time they can combine work with enjoying their visit.'[45] About 40,000 people a year take part in the scheme and very large numbers of them have provided care for elderly and disabled people both in private homes and institutional settings. The scheme was expanded in August 2003 to allow people to work in their professions and to transfer more easily to a work permit after one year. This may reduce the numbers entering low-paid domestic work or just increase the total numbers using the scheme overall.

Britain, like many other countries both rich and poor, has been able to attract migrants to take low-paid, low-skilled jobs. Thus, it has a much larger domestic workforce than if it were dependent only on British nationals. British families are able to afford childcare and cleaning services because of the circumstances that force these people to leave their homes thousands of miles away to look for work. The global economic system creates the context for the paid domestic labour market, even though its workings are played out, at the most intimate scale, within people's homes. The precise way in which states recruit domestic workers and consider their work is very important in determining how those workers are treated within the homes they care for. The specific nature of visa regulations can protect domestic workers and help them find good jobs with decent employers, or it can leave them open to the most horrific forms of abuse. Migrant labour is exceedingly important within Britain for supplying domestic workers in private homes and other low-paid workers to related 'caring' jobs. As the next chapter sets out, the pressures on families to employ domestic help have been increasing at just the same time as the supply of low-skilled female labour is drying up.

3 | 'Carefree' Britain

This chapter explores the trends that have encouraged the growth of domestic employment in Britain in detail. It examines recent changes in women's working patterns including their increasing inclusion in the long-hours culture and in jobs demanding high levels of commitment. It also looks at how changes in work practices have affected men, making them employers of domestic labour too. It then explores how growing income inequalities have underpinned an increase in the demand for and the supply of domestic help.

Women: the new professional and flexible workforce

Explanations for the growth of paid domestic work in many parts of the world have focused on women's increasing participation in paid employment: they are unable to carry out the childcare (and sometimes elder care) that was traditionally their full-time role. The swell of women into paid work outside the home has, of course, been an important element of the changing context within which domestic work now takes place but its impact is more complicated than just a simple equation of more women working equals more demand for private childcare. It is necessary to look at the ways in which women now work: their hours, jobs and rates of pay, and to look at how attitudes towards the home change when women go out to work. It is not the case that women have never traditionally worked outside the home – many women have, and have worked long hours in arduous jobs. What has happened more recently is that middle-class women have begun to work whilst still retaining responsibility for maintaining a home that is a status symbol.

Trends in women's employment

Women have always worked, both inside and outside the home. The 1950s ideal of the nuclear family supported by a male breadwinner was only a reality for a minority of families and for a very short amount of time. Even then it had to be supported by government intervention in pay rates and 'marriage bans' for most jobs that kept married women out of work. However, today there are more women in paid employment, more women work full time, more women work long hours and many more women with young children are employed. In addition, more women are now in professional and 'career-structured' jobs than ever before. This means women are earning more but also that the penalties for career breaks are greater.

Since the 1950s women's participation in paid work outside the home has been increasing, reaching 69.6 per cent in Spring 2003 (the equivalent rate for men was 79 per cent).[1] In 1959 just under 50 per cent of women were employed and this rose slowly during the 1960s to plateau at around 60 per cent between 1973 and 1981. In the early 1980s there was actually a slight dip in the proportion of women in employment before another period of steady growth in the late 1980s and throughout the 1990s.[2] From 1971 until the 1980s, while more women did join the workforce, they were largely in part-time jobs, particularly 'short' part-time work that involved relatively few hours and tended to be very low paid with few benefits and little security. According to Catherine Hakim, in fact, in terms of full-time work or the total number of hours worked there was no increase at all in women's employment in Britain between 1971 and 1980.[3] During the 1980s women's part-time work continued to grow, bolstered by the growth in low-paid service work and the differential rights given to part-time workers at the time which made them cheaper to employ and easier to sack. Since 1992 another 1.39 million women have joined the workforce to bring women's employment rates to record levels. Now 45 per cent of all those employed in Britain are women and Britain has the third-highest rates of female economic activity in the EU (behind only Denmark and Sweden).[4] In the period since 1959 male employment rates have declined from near 95 per cent to under 80 per cent.

Much of the increase in women's employment in recent years has been made up by women who have children joining the workforce, and particularly women with young children entering paid work. In Spring 2003, 65 per cent of all women with dependent children were in paid work. Women with children of secondary school age had rates of employment close to men's – 78 per cent against 79 per cent for all men. And women with children of this age were more likely to be working than women without dependent children. For those with young children, participation rates were lower, at 52 per cent, 67 per cent of whom were in part-time work. However, these numbers show an increase in recent years. In 1990 the number of married or co-habiting women with children under school age who were employed was 45 per cent, by 2002 it was nearly 60 per cent. Single women with dependent children are less likely to work, but their rates of employment have also increased sharply. In 2002 60 per cent of all single mothers were in work (against 68 per cent of single women without children) and about 33 per cent of single mothers with children under 5 years old were in employment.[5]

What this means for the women doing this work can vary immensely depending on their class. For middle-class women, the chance to work, even when children are young, can mean the return to a fulfilling job, the chance to continue up the career ladder without a break or to be taken seriously in comparison to male colleagues. For poorer women with dependent children and lower skills or educational attainment, work is more likely to be a necessity, the result of a decline in real male wages, male employment and marriage. Work is more likely to mean part-time, unfulfilling work, fitted in around childcare or other family commitments. Both of these feed into the domestic employment mix, one on the demand side, the other supplying a potential workforce.

Women – the new rich?

Whilst most of the growth in women's employment has been in part-time and low-paid work, there has been a dramatic increase in the numbers of women who work in well-paid jobs, including those that demand long hours. In 2002 31 per cent of all managers and senior officials were women, including 29 per cent of corporate managers, 40 per cent of those in occupations classed as 'professional' – such as lawyers, accountants, doctors and researchers – were women as were 45 per cent of people in occupations classed as 'associate professional and technical', which includes nurses, police officers, speech therapists and physiotherapists, along with many other jobs that require quite a high level of professional training.[6] Women still earn less than men and are much less likely to be found in the highest grades of their professions or in positions of power in large companies, but there are some women at these levels, and increasing numbers of them who are high earners. Between 1979 and 1995 the top 10 per cent of full-time female workers in Britain saw their pay increase by 69.5 per cent in real terms (the equivalent figure for men was 48.6 per cent).[7] Women's earnings are particularly important in accounting for any increase in paid domestic work because many households make decisions about whether to employ help, particularly childcare, by comparing the cost of it just to the woman's pay. In other words if childcare costs as much or nearly as much as the woman in a family would earn by working for the hours the childcare covers it is seen to be too costly, regardless of what the total household income is. If male incomes rose but women's did not fewer families would think it was financially worthwhile to pay for a nanny or au pair, and would make different decisions about childcare. Childcare is rarely seen as helping both men and women to work.

It is the increase in the number of women entering professional and well-paid work that is the real change in women's employment. Working-class women have always worked in large numbers (often as the servants of the rich), as we have seen. What is different now is that some women are now earning high salaries and that middle-class women, with quite different expectations and assumptions about their lives and their work, are now working. This, of course, has more of an impact on rates and patterns of domestic employment than any amount of growth in the numbers of low-paid or unskilled feminized jobs. Not only can well-paid women afford to pay for help in the home or childcare, they are more likely to have homes or lifestyles that take large amounts of labour to support.

The movement of women into well-paid and higher-status work has meant an increasing number of women are in what can be termed 'career-structured' jobs. These are jobs which allow for promotion and progression over time both within an individual situation and by moving between posts and employers. For such women the penalties, in terms of life-long loss of earnings and opportunities, are much greater should they take a break from such work or go part time.

Long hours in the new work order

This entry into professional and career-structured jobs has also meant that more women, and for the first time, middle-class women – those who could afford to employ and would want to employ domestic help – are exposed to the long hours culture of the modern British workplace. Working hours have been on the increase across the board in Britain and are now the longest in Europe. From the end of the nineteenth century until the 1970s working hours declined and it was assumed that this trend would continue, supported by new technologies, giving everyone more leisure. In the 1980s, however, the trend reversed and, as the proportion of people in employment decreased, the working hours of those with full-time jobs went up. Instead of work being shared between people, giving everyone a balance of work and leisure, the 1980s saw fewer people doing more and more work and increasingly defining themselves through that work.[8] Caring is being squeezed out of people's lives by their working hours.

In Britain the average full-time working week is now around 45 hours, and is only that short because of the restrictions placed on working hours by the European Working Time Directive. When this was introduced in 1998, it was thought that there were 4.5 million people in Britain working more than the 48 hours a week it allowed.[9] In the United States average working hours are longer still, and holiday entitlements about half of those ensured for European workers. It has been calculated that the average American now works the equivalent of an extra month every year compared to their counterparts in 1948.

Long working hours have spread into middle-class and professional jobs in both the public and private sectors. In her book *Having None of It: Women, Men and the Future of Work*, Suzanne Franks recounts examples of excessive hours being worked by doctors, social workers and teachers as well as lawyers and bankers.[10] For many these long hours have been accompanied by a culture of 'presenteeism', the need to be seen at your desk for longer and longer durations. Increasingly, it seems that people's value and commitment at work has been judged on the number of hours they are prepared to work, or to be present in their workplace, rather than the quality of the work they do. Penelope Leach has described this practice as 'American masochism – putting yourself through a pointless and unproductive period of work at the end of the day to prove to your superiors that you are prepared to undertake tasks that you do not want or have to do'.[11]

In *The Time Bind: When Work Becomes Home and Home Becomes Work*, Arlie Russell Hochschild exposes the logic driving this long hours culture. In her book she examines working practices in an American company which, on paper, has some of the best work–life balance policies around. She shows that even in an environment that appears to understand the potential benefits of facilitating work for parents, long hours and total commitment to the company are taken as the norm. While office-based employees are generally contracted to work 40 hours a week, 'normal' working hours are assumed by all to be at least 50. A manager who has negotiated a 32-hour 'part-time' week does this in order to spend 'only' 45 hours a week at her desk, plus another 5–10 working at home or from her car. The logic underpinning this attitude towards work is revealed in a conversation reported to Hochschild, between Eileen, a highly qualified engineer who wants to work part time, and her boss.

> He said to me 'Eileen, I don't know how to do part time. My experience is that people who put in the hours are the one's who succeed.' I

said, 'Measure me on my results.' He said, 'No. It doesn't work that way. What matters is how much time you put into the job, not the volume of work.'[12]

This attitude, valuing the hours people will put in rather than the work they could do, prevailed throughout the company, even with the head of personnel, who was responsible for implementing work–life balance policies! While it might seem astonishing that a manager could articulate a position like this, Hochschild demonstrates that the company she studied is in no way unusual and was in fact rated as a 'good' employer compared to most others. Such attitudes were justified by managers in terms of commitment to a 'team' of colleagues, in maintaining relationships, or being seen to pull one's weight. Often, employees were characterized as letting down their workmates if they did not want to work excessive hours, rather than being seen as quite reasonably resisting the company's attempts to dominate every part and moment of their lives.

Such attitudes towards working hours and towards the place work should have in people's lives were developed with the assumption that people who 'worked' did not have responsibilities outside of work for childcare, housekeeping and the like. They are often maintained by a layer of male senior managers who do have someone else to take care of all their needs and worries beyond the workplace. When women take on jobs that demand total commitment to work and long hours, they tend to do so on male terms and would rather pay another woman to fill the gaps at home than challenge either the gender division of labour at home or the excessive and unnecessary demands of work. No one wants to be thought of as unable to cope.

Flexible working practices and the use of new technologies have had the tendency to spread work into all parts of our lives rather than facilitating ways of working that fit better with home. More people than ever before, including more parents, work non-standard hours, responding both to the demands of a 24-hour society and to doing business across time zones in a globalized business environment. While some people have been able to use flexible working practices to find a way to negotiate the demands of home and work, more often the 'flexibility' demanded of employees is really total dedication. As one worker in a Cambridge high tech firm put it 'flexibility is the flexibility to work on a problem 24 hours a day'.[13] People are expected to be available to clients whenever they are needed, no matter which time zone they are in, to be able to travel at short notice and never to be off duty. Technology means that people can check e-mail from home, receive faxes in their car or be at the end of a mobile phone line even when they are on holiday, that is if they get to take a holiday. The Daycare Trust has documented what they call 'the rise of the shift parent'. They have found that 34 per cent of working families contain a parent who worked weekends, 22 per cent contained a parent who worked shifts and 18 per cent of women with children in two-parent families regularly work evenings. Women with young children are much more likely to work unsocial hours than those without.[14]

All of these practices make combining work with other responsibilities extremely difficult. Long and unpredictable working hours create a demand for equally flexible forms of childcare, which are rarely met by public or private sector nurseries or out of school clubs. It is easy to see how long working hours translate into demand for nannies, au pairs and other forms of private childcare. However, long working hours, particularly for women, also create demand for housekeeping services. As the time spent at work grows, time outside work becomes more and more precious and well-paid professionals seek to buy back their leisure time by paying for other people to do cleaning, ironing and the like. As people commit more and more of their lives to work they also adopt a moral framework that puts paid work above other activities and values things in terms of monetary rewards. This not only provides a logic for employing domestic help – it's cheaper than doing the cleaning yourself if you could be working more and earning more – it promotes a self-reinforcing view of domestic labour which sees it as lacking value precisely because it is unrewarded. In a world where everything is judged on what it earns or what it costs, housework has a very low status indeed and there is all the more reason to get someone else to do it.

Men, work and housework

Of course it is not only women who could do housework and childcare, and it is not only their changing working patterns that affect who employs domestic help. If men took on traditional female roles or even shared equally in the work that needs to be done around the home, there would probably be a lot less paid help employed. However, while women's experiences of work outside the home have changed dramatically in the past 50 years, men's attitudes to work inside the home have shifted much less and public expectations of women's responsibility for home and children have endured untouched.

Study after study has demonstrated that despite women's increased work outside the home, men have not become much more likely to carry out tasks inside the home. Women who work full time, on average do nine hours a week more housework than their partners. They do more housework if they work longer hours than their partners and they do more housework than their partners even if those partners are unemployed.[15] Latest UK government figures show that on average men do an hour and 20 minutes less housework a day than women, and that does not include childcare or shopping. Forty per cent of men do no ironing or laundry, while less than 5 per cent of women do not do these tasks.[16] The average woman spends about three times as long doing childcare and about four times as long doing housework as the average man each day, despite only spending 30 per cent less time, an hour and fifteen minutes, in her main job.[17]

Women have remained overwhelmingly responsible for housework and childcare, whether they do it themselves, pay for someone else to do it, or manage to persuade other household members to take some of it on. Men are often thought of as 'helping out' if they run round with the Hoover or put on a load of washing, rather than being seen as doing tasks which are quite obviously their job too. The responsibility for organizing the home and childcare can become arduous when children need to be taken to the dentists or dropped at a friend's, or when deliveries are due at home or the boiler packs up. Organizing the smooth running of a home can involve large amounts of work and worry, most of which is even more invisible than physical housework tasks. And this type of organizational work – worrying about whether childcare arrangements will match up, caring about whether there's any milk in the fridge – is the work which men are least likely to take on, no matter how much they 'help out' around the house.

But just sharing housework between men and women will not solve the problem of how to create enough hours to do all the care work that needs to be done (although it would help a lot!). Men are subject to the same long hours and flexible work culture that has increasingly engulfed women. In fact men seem to be much less resistant to demands for increased hours at work than women are. Women have more often sought a balance between time and pay, whereas men are rarely prepared to consider a shorter working week if it would mean lower pay. Men are more likely to define themselves through their work and to see long hours as a status symbol, indicating the significance of their job and the importance of their role.[18]

Men are also more likely to increase their working hours when they have young children, seeing their role as a father as one which involves providing financial resources more than anything else, and this is a role that can be reinforced by social expectations. A recent government study found that very long hours (60 or more a week) were 'particularly prevalent among . . . men in households with children'.[19] In Britain, men with children work longer hours than men without children and the longest hours of men anywhere in Europe.[20] Figures from the USA show that only 4 per cent of men with children under 12 years old worked less than 40 hours a week and very few men, with or without children, expressed a desire for shorter working hours. For some men it is precisely their role as fathers that pushes them to work these hours. As Hochschild reports from her interviews with fathers, this can be the result of a desire to make up for perceived failings in their own fathers or to match their fathers' attitudes. As one manager, who had not taken *any* leave, i.e. not even a single day of holiday, for the first six years of his child's life, and who worked, in his own words, 'incredibly long hours' explained:

> I was the youngest of six kids, the only one to go to college. My father was a machinist on the railroad in Peoria, Illinois. When I was in high school, he was laid off from work. It was a crushing experience for him and for me. I wanted to do it differently.[21]

The result of this 'doing it differently' was to enslave himself to his company and to give only in financial terms to his family. When he became a manager he created an environment that forced others to behave in the same way, hardly a less crushing experience for all their families.

For other men long hours are taken on as a way to earn more to pay for the things it is imagined make up the perfect home. But they can also be a way of escaping the demands and tensions that young children can bring. As a self-confessed 'overtime hound' told Hochschild:

> I take all the overtime I can get, all the doubles I can stand. I'm an overtime hound. There's a rule about working more than fifteen consecutive hours, but once in a while I'll pop a twenty-four or a twenty-five hour at a go. . . . Most of my buddies will settle for forty hours and say 'See you later.' But they're buddies without kids. If I had no kids I'd work forty hours, too. . . . I work around 50 percent for need, 25 percent for greed. A lot of it is greed. And 25 percent is getting away from the house.[22]

With attitudes like this prevailing amongst men, and constant demands on men to display their machismo by working longer and longer hours, it is clear that it is not they who are going to be making up for any domestic work that women cannot do. Men may do more childcare now than their fathers, be prepared to change nappies or take the kids to the park, but they are not likely to be providing all the care their children need.

Men's working hours, and their attitudes to work outside the home and the work that needs doing inside the home, can be just as important in creating a demand for paid help as women's increasing participation in paid work. Whilst few employing families will think of paid help as directly replacing men's labour in the home, men create demand for paid help for both childcare and housework.

Long and increasing work hours and a work culture that demands total commitment mean that men's and women's work habits together make the employment of a nanny or au pair seem like the only way childcare and work can be negotiated. Men are unlikely to take leave from work to provide childcare when normal arrangements break down. They find it difficult to take time off when children are ill or have medical appointments. They may find it hard to leave work early (or on time) if a childminder is on holiday and a child needs picking up from school. All of this means that private, highly flexible childcare arrangements are increasingly attractive. If two parents work long hours in environments that are unsympathetic to their home lives the childcare options that are available are very limited. If one parent can work flexibly and cover if gaps arise in normal arrangements, there are many more options that might work.

Men also create demand for cleaning and housekeeping services simply by not doing that work themselves. In a survey of dual career households, Nicky Gregson and Michelle Lowe found that couples who shared housework were much less likely to hire a cleaner than couples with similar jobs and earnings where the woman was expected to do all the work. In these households the women often explained their decision to employ a cleaner as a way of 'stopping the arguments' with partners who did not see housework as their problem.[23] Barbara Ehrenreich reports that marriage counsellors even advise couples to hire domestic help as an alternative to squabbling over who does the chores. And the owner of a cleaning franchise she interviewed said he gets customers by calling on a Saturday morning, because it is the 'prime time for arguing over the fact the house is a mess'.[24]

Single men who live alone or with groups of friends are much more likely to employ cleaners or to use help, such as an ironing service, than single women are. For a start, men do earn more than women and are, therefore, more often going to find domestic help easily affordable. Men are also more likely to think that they do not know how to do housework or to think that it is a waste of time. The numbers of single person households has grown dramatically in the last 20 years, as has the number of households made up of independent adults living together. Much of this growth comes from young professionals who are geographically mobile, leaving home to follow work. Instead of taking the washing home at weekends, or living with mum so as to be well looked after, young men are turning to paid domestic services instead. Of course, single men do look after themselves most of the time and most are quite capable of ironing a shirt and cleaning the toilet.

But there are large numbers of others who are replacing their mothers' attentions with those of a paid cleaner, rather than doing the work themselves.

Income inequalities: the winners and losers in a global economy

Long and increasing working hours and persistent inequalities in responsibility for housework and childcare are one aspect of the situation within which paid domestic employment has grown. Another part of the picture is not the differences between men and women but the differences between rich and poor. The last chapter showed how income differences on a global scale have caused flows of domestic workers around the world. Extremes of wealth and poverty also characterize modern British society, particularly in the largest cities, and provide a situation where some people find it very easy to purchase the labour of others. Low incomes, particularly dependence on welfare benefits, create a ready supply of domestic workers, willing to take on cash-in-hand work, hidden from the authorities. High incomes for the 'winners' in the global economy mean more conspicuous consumption, larger homes, lavish lifestyles and the desire to employ others to do the dirty work.

Income inequality and neo-liberalism

Around the world there seems to be a pattern of wealth flowing from poor to rich. Poor countries pay the rich far more in debt servicing than they receive in aid or foreign investment and at a smaller scale, within countries and cities, the richer have been getting richer and the poor poorer. David Harvey reports that between 1960 and 1991 the share of global income owned by the richest 20 per cent of the world's population rose from 70 per cent to 85 per cent while at the same time the poorest 20 per cent of the population saw their share fall from 2.3 per cent to just 1.4 per cent. In 1991 more than 85 per cent of the world's population shared only 15 per cent of its income. The super-super-rich, the 358 dollar billionaires, had a net worth equal to the combined income of the poorest 45 per cent of the *world's* population (2.3 billion people). And Bill Gates, one of the richest men on the planet, had a net worth in 1995 which was alone greater than the combined net worth of the poorest 40 per cent of Americans (106 million people).[25]

It is no wonder that in conditions of such gross inequality the rich employ the poor as servants in increasing numbers. David Harvey goes on to compare the working conditions in modern sweatshops to those that existed in Britain when Marx and Engels were writing the Communist Manifesto and servant employment was booming. In Marx's time it was recorded that the milliner Mary Anne Walkley regularly worked 30-hour shifts without a break and died at 20 years of age after a particularly hard spell at work 'preparing magnificent dresses for the noble ladies invited to a ball in honour of the newly imported Princess of Wales'.[26] Yet, inequalities between rich and poor are greater now than they were even then. Thousands of women work in appalling conditions, not unlike those that Mary Anne Walkley would have known, but today those women live on other continents and the products they make are the brands we all know well, rather than just luxuries for the nobility.

Income inequalities within countries have also increased in recent decades. In the United States the richest 1 per cent of households own 40 per cent of the wealth.[27] In the UK the richest 5 per cent of individuals owned more than 40 per cent of marketable wealth, with the poorest half of the population having just 6 per cent of the wealth in 2000. If the value of housing is taken out of the equation, this picture of the UK is even more unequal. The richest 1 per cent of individuals owns 32 per cent of the wealth and the poorest 50 per cent of the population have only 1 per cent between them. The figures show growing inequality over time. In 1976 the wealthiest 1 per cent of the population had 29 per cent of the wealth and the poorest 50 per cent had 12 percent of the total. The greatest gains have been made by those in the richest 10 per cent. In 1976 this group had 57 per cent of UK wealth and by 2000 this was up to 72 per cent.[28]

London: a consuming capital?

In London, the part of Britain where employing domestic help seems to be most common,[29] the gap between rich and poor appears to be even more pronounced. In the last two decades the number of high earners in London has grown, as has the size of their earnings. There is also a larger professional middle-class in London: 30 per cent of the population of the capital have a degree or professional qualification, compared with 23 per cent in the rest of the country.[30] At the same time traditional skilled working-class jobs have disappeared or relocated, leaving more people in very low-paid unskilled work, or dependent on government benefits. Since the mid 1970s London has consistently been getting richer than the rest of the country. Average incomes of individuals and households are higher in London and there are about 50 per cent more households in London with high incomes (over £750 a week) than in the rest of the UK. However, at the other end of the scale, households with very low incomes (under £100 a week) exist in the same proportion in London as they do in the UK as a whole. In fact between 1981 and 1999 the proportion of Londoners in the lowest income category increased slightly.[31]

The importance of London as a global financial centre has increased the numbers of people on very large salaries and big bonuses. Many of the industries which command the highest salaries – financial, legal and business services such as advertising and PR – are concentrated in London and in the City more specifically. For those in finance, the globalization of financial markets has driven salaries upwards. Top traders are now paid millions of pounds a year and many other City workers earn over £100,000. Starting salaries for new graduates in City financial and legal firms are typically over £40,000 a year, rising to £80,000 in four years, i.e. for a 25-year-old. Bonuses for junior analysts could be as much as £50,000 a year on top of a salary, rising to £200,000 for traders, and up to £4 million for directors who perform well.[32]

London also contains one of the highest concentrations of deprivation in England. Out of 343 local authorities in England, five of the ten most deprived and 13 of the 20 most deprived are in London. Poverty and deprivation are particularly concentrated in inner London, which has higher levels of unemployment and benefit dependency than the country as a whole, with a quarter of all households receiving family credit or income support and over a third of all households receiving housing benefit.[33]

It is not hard to see that the concentration of wealth in the hands of a few and the relative poverty of the many could facilitate the growth of domestic employment. As Ehrenreich so eloquently puts it, in a society with income inequalities like these 'the degradation of others is easily purchased'.[34] Income inequalities feed into the domestic labour market in various ways. As the incomes of some people grow they can easily afford to pay for other people to provide services for them. Those services may be manicures or massages or they might be gardening and cleaning. When people have very low incomes they are more likely to take on work that is unattractive – e.g. because it is physically hard, unpleasant or degrading – than people who have other options. These people may be the poor of the world, not just of the city, and they may have left jobs they trained for in their home countries to take on much less attractive work as domestic helpers for the global rich far from home. Or they may be amongst the existing poor within a particular city. Beyond the simple economics of supply and demand there are also more subtle ways in which such unequal incomes feed the growth of domestic employment.

Benefit dependency and the poverty trap

The benefit system in Britain works in such a way that it creates a supply of labour for part-time, live-out, cash-in-hand cleaning jobs and effectively subsidizes the employment of cleaners by middle-class families. Most benefits are paid only to people who officially do not work, or who work for very limited hours for low pay. This fact provides an incentive for some people to hide their work from the official gaze.

For most means tested benefits, claimants are only allowed to work a certain number of hours a week. If they work more hours, they risk all their benefits being stopped, even if their earnings are lower than the benefits they would lose. Income Support, for example, is only paid to people who work for less than 16 hours a week and whose income is below a set level. Receiving income support also gives people access to housing benefit and other benefits such as free prescriptions or free school meals for their children. If someone on Income Support took on a couple of hours of extra week each week, or took work at a higher rate of pay, they would lose their entitlements to most of these benefits. For each extra hour that they worked they could lose as much money (or nearly as much money) in benefits.

This situation creates a 'poverty trap' whereby it is increasingly difficult for people to enter the paid workforce because of the benefits they would lose. The trap is deepest for those people whose benefits are relatively high but whose capacity to work is reduced. For example, lone parents receive slightly higher benefits than non-parents between the ages of 18 and 25 and get allowances for each of their children, but they are often restricted in the hours they can work because of their childcare responsibilities. One short-term solution for those trapped on benefits is to work 'cash-in-hand' so as not to impinge on benefit entitlement. Cash-in-hand jobs are very variable and not all are low paid or involve manual work, as might be imagined.[35] However, one source of informal work that is readily available to many people is domestic, particularly cleaning, work.[36] Employers of cleaners prefer to keep transactions informal so they do not have to pay tax or National Insurance contributions and so they do not have to worry about the implications of employment legislation. Cleaners like the fact that they can work in a flexible manner without losing any benefits. Domestic work is well hidden from view and therefore relatively safe from detection.

In addition women find it easy to get cleaning jobs and lone parents find the arrangement of the work particularly attractive. Most employers ask for, and will check references, but other formalities, such as application forms, or qualifications are just not used. It is assumed that all women know how to clean, so cleaners rarely have to prove their skills to get work. Also most employers want cleaning done during the middle of the day when they are out. This means cleaning can fit particularly well with childcare. Cleaners can work during the day but still be there to pick the kids up from school. Likewise the flexible and informal nature of cleaning work means that most cleaners can cancel or rearrange a job if their child is ill or has a dentist's appointment. Cleaning in the informal sector allows benefit-dependent women to earn enough money to improve their standard of living in the short hours they have available. Many lone parents in particular find there is no formal sector work that does this: they simply cannot earn enough in the time they have to make up for lost benefits.

While some people are surprised that cleaning is not as badly paid as some jobs – cleaners in London, for example, could expect to take home nearly twice the minimum wage – cleaners' wages are in fact subsidized by their state benefits and many employers can afford to employ a cleaner because they do not have to pay all other possible costs involved. The state benefits act as a safety net. They mean that periods when cleaners cannot work, for example, due to illness (their own or their children's) or to not being able to arrange any or enough work, do not automatically plunge them into having no income at all. As a result, the wages that employers pay do not need to cover these risks. Some employers do pay sick pay and holiday pay but many more do not and nor does the average weekly rate earned allow cleaners to save enough to cover these periods.

Cleaners normally have limits on the hours they can work because of their childcare responsibilities, the logistics of fitting in and travelling to a large number of different houses in a single day, and the physical demands of the work. All of these factors mean that many cleaners are part time, working for anything from 5 to 30 hours a week. On top of this cleaners may have periods when they have no work or less work than they want.

As well as having to cater for their own children during holidays, or to cope with other demands from their families, cleaners usually work for a number of employers and their hours and commitments can change quite frequently as people move house, have children, change their working hours or just change their minds about the amount of cleaning they want done. This means there can be substantial variations in cleaners' earnings throughout a year. All of this flexibility is made possible because of the benefits safety net. Cleaners want to work to get themselves and their families out of poverty, just as the government says they should, but they find it impossible to work in the formal sector because of the low wages available, the inflexibility of most jobs and the lack of affordable childcare.[37]

Many employers like to think of their cleaners as 'self-employed', responsible for their own taxes and for taking on the risks of illness, unemployment or short hours – the way a painter and decorator or mobile hairdresser might. The amount that cleaners are paid, however, is much more similar to that of a low-skilled employee whose holidays and other benefits are provided by their employer, rather than a self-employed worker whose hourly rate takes account of the risks they have. Both employers and cleaners themselves talk about how relatively well paid cleaning can be when they compare its hourly rate to other jobs. However, weekly, monthly or yearly earnings of cleaners are rarely thought about, because jobs are negotiated by the hour and employers will not necessarily be aware of how many other jobs cleaners have. People might find it easy to understand that a lawyer's hourly rate takes into account the hours that they cannot bill for, or that a freelance journalist has to make enough in the time they do work to cover the times that they cannot, but few people think about cleaners' earnings this way. The gap is filled by state benefits, which relieves employers from the need to think about the times when cleaners cannot work and which therefore keeps overall rates of pay down and makes paid domestic help more affordable to larger numbers of people. When the press or the government talk about 'benefit fraud' they rarely frame middle-class households as beneficiaries of that fraud.

Lavish lifestyles

There are many forms of domestic labour and some of these are encouraged when the earnings of those at the top of the scale increase. The boom in pay and bonuses in places like the City of London have been widely associated with a culture of conspicuous consumption. This extreme wealth and its public display was perhaps most decisively demonstrated in newspaper reports of six investment bankers from the City running up a bill of £44,000 for a single meal at the restaurant Petrus in July 2001. This bill included three bottles of wine costing £11,000 each and another costing £9,200. The restaurant actually threw in the £300 cost of the meal for free! The bankers were all male, 25–35 years old and worked for the investment banking division of a major bank. The bank claimed that it was a private meal being paid for by the bankers themselves, not by the firm, but that perhaps revealed even more clearly the phenomenal levels of disposable income available to some City employees.[38]

Much of this wealth is also channelled into property and this has been an important factor in driving up housing costs in London and other cities. One outcome of this is that some people have larger houses which are decorated and maintained in a way that demands large amounts of labour – other people's labour. This might start with the employment of an interior design firm to restyle a home, but it is likely to end in the routine employment of cleaning and other domestic staff, to keep it looking just so. People who know that they can afford to employ others to do the cleaning are also unlikely to consider how much work a particular décor scheme might take to keep looking stylish and they can choose interiors that are particularly labour-intensive to maintain. These might include having lots of objects on display that have to be carefully dusted. Pale-coloured carpets or flooring, or extensive use of traditional materials such as wood and ceramic tiles, can all create work. Whereas someone who does their own housework and ironing might think twice about whether a new plate will go in the dishwasher or whether a new top is likely to crease, those who know they can pay someone to do these jobs can create a lifestyle that takes much more labour to maintain.

As well as the labour involved in maintaining a conspicuously affluent house, there are other consumption activities, such as entertaining and shopping, that can create a demand for domestic help. Hosts wanting to impress their friends may use catering services for large parties but people who regularly entertain at home can choose to employ more permanent help to do this. This may be in the form of having a full-time cook or a 'housekeeper/cook' who lives in and has multiple duties, or it may be by getting the au pair or nanny to help out with preparation and serving. However it is organized, hosting parties and dinner parties can create a substantial amount of work, and it may be a decisive factor for some families when they opt to employ full-time or live-in help rather than having a part-time cleaner and/or using collective childcare at a local nursery.

Buying exclusive products and services can involve someone else waiting for deliveries or to let builders in. For some people this reinforces their desire to have full-time help present to deal with these arrangements, but it has also created demand for a new kind of domestic service: the 'concierge'. Based on the ideal of living in a serviced flat or hotel with a 24-hour doorman, these services will do things like letting people into your house for maintenance, collecting dry cleaning or arranging flowers for a friend's birthday. Some offer travel or restaurant booking, personal shoppers and even lifestyle coaching. One British concierge service advertises 'Proactive work/life assistance – 247365 personal lifestyle support.'[39] *The Which? Guide to Domestic Help* reported in 1998 that:

> Young professionals in UK cities spend a good deal of money on domestic help. One agency quotes the example of a 25-year old money broker in London who said he wanted someone to do everything his mother did for him when he lived at home. Once the agency had established that this did not include bathing him or wiping his nose, it was more than happy to provide someone to cook, clean, iron, shop, sign for the post and deliveries, pay the milkman, organize repairs and

decorating and attend to every other practical domestic detail of the young man's life.[40]

These services are provided by some employers for their employees and are marketed at people who are too busy to run their own lives, people with lifestyles that need 'support' presumably. They all help people to consume more – more goods, more travel and more personal services. The implication is that some people simply do not have time to spend all the money they earn and need assistance to do it.

Stark income inequalities in cities like London have created the bizarre situation where people with so much money that they need help to spend it can live just streets away from people who can find no way of escaping poverty. The high-maintenance lifestyles of the rich can create the only kind of work that the poor, trapped on benefits, can do.

Who cares?

This growth in wealth at the top of the hierarchy – the rise of the 'work rich' and the retrenchment of the plain old rich – has fed demand for many forms of domestic employment as well as underpinning the development of new forms of domestic service. The last 20 years has seen the growth of a range of new forms of domestic and personal services. Along with the concierge or 'lifestyle manager' already mentioned there have been increases in enterprises such as ironing services, school run services (which pick your children up from home and deliver them to school the way a public school bus might once have done) and myriad delivery services such as those which deliver pre-cooked frozen meals to your door, all there to help those who have lifestyles that they are prepared to pay others to maintain.

While this area has been booming, however, the traditional care workforce has been in decline, causing crises in both the public and private sectors. There are approximately 204,000 people in Britain who are employed to provide care for people in their own homes; this includes childcare, and care for elderly, disabled and vulnerable adults.[41] There are also carers in nurseries and playgroups and working in hospitals, residential homes and day centres. This domestic care sector has been under increasing stress as the number of people needing care has increased and the workforce has been unable to expand fast enough to keep up. The shortage of staff in many types of care work, however, is not simply a result of fewer people training or others leaving the sector for different jobs; it is the logical result of broad-scale social attitudes towards care, its value and the worth of the people who do it. As a society the value that we place on care work, and care workers, is so low that almost any other service seems more important.

Demand for domestic care services has grown for a number of reasons. First, there are more old people, and more very old people (those over 85, who tend to have greater need of care). Because families are more dispersed, however, they are less able to provide care for members themselves. Women's roles and aspirations have changed, making them less likely to take on the unpaid care of young and old family members, but there has been a reluctance to accept men as suitable carers or, indeed, for men to want to take on this work. At the same time as families are less and less able to provide care themselves, institutional care for the old, sick or vulnerable has also decreased, meaning that private, paid-for care for people in their own homes is growing fast.[42]

Traditionally, paid home carers have been low-skilled, working-class women who entered the sector because it was seen as suitable 'women's work' and because they had few alternatives. However, as women have become more highly educated and more widely involved in paid employment there is an increasing range of work that is recognized as suitable and attainable for them and there is no longer a substantial pool of carers available. In fact, one academic commentator has stated that overall changes in the shape of the working population mean that any sector which currently relies on poorly qualified young women to fill posts will have to improve the quality of jobs to make them suitable for a more educated workforce or 'rapidly end up in a severe labour supply shortage'.[43]

The status of domestic work and care work in home and institutional settings is very low, as are average wages. This lack of recognition and remuneration helps to demoralize workers and prevents others from joining the sector. Much of the work that carers and domestic workers do is considered to be unskilled and the knowledge and qualities needed to do it go unrecognized. The importance of the work, to the people being cared for, their families and society more generally, is rarely considered. Many care workers earn little over minimum wage and both childcare and domestic care for the elderly are among the ten lowest-paid occupations in the UK.

While the rich have been steadily getting richer in a deregulated economy, the neo-liberal approach to welfare and the public sector has devalued services and driven wages in the whole care sector even lower. The context within which domestic care workers' wages are set is influenced by two quite different sets of thinking, both of which work to keep pay and status low. First, the institutional care sector affects the general level of care workers' pay because of its importance as an employer. In recent years pressure on local authority budgets has led to 'cost containment', and costs for local authorities have been held at 1992 levels. This means there have been tight restrictions on who is entitled to care, with the number of people receiving care dropping by 28 per cent since 1992, and wages have not kept pace with inflation.[44] This creates a general atmosphere where home carers are under-valued and underpaid and increasingly likely to leave the sector.

The second important input has to do with the way that the value of care and other domestic work is calculated within households. Because most domestic work is done for free by household members, it is generally considered to have no value. When imagining how much it would be worth to pay someone to do something for us, we tend to think about what it would cost us to buy an alternative. Often, for domestic work, the calculation is that the other person's labour would be worth nothing to us because we could do the same tasks ourselves for free. This is obviously not a great starting point for calculating a good rate of pay. Sometimes, however, domestic labour does have a cost and this is normally when it prevents someone from doing paid work. Childcare is the clear example of this. In this situation, most households consider how much the member undertaking the childcare could earn in the time available if they were freed of their childcare responsibilities and they use this to help calculate what they would be prepared pay for childcare. In most families it is the mother's time that is thought about in this way, both because women are more like to be considered as primary childcarers and because women earn less than men on average and are therefore seen as taking less out of the household if they give up paid work.

The assumptions underlying these calculations by individual families are devastating to the value placed on care work and care workers. Care is only seen as worth paying for if it costs less than another person's earnings. Additionally, care workers' pay has to be held below not just average pay but *women's* pay, which is already 20 per cent below the combined male and female average.

Care workers often have to work longer hours than the people they work for in order to cover their employers' travel times and handovers at the beginning and end of the day. It is not unusual for a nanny to have to be at work from before eight in the morning until after seven at night. This means that their hourly rate of pay must be still lower than that of their employer because more hours of work need to be paid for. All of this thinking conspires to cast care work as low status and low value.

Even when carers are qualified and recognized as excellent at their work, that work is still seen as worth less than whatever their employer does. This is not the result of individual employers consciously devaluing the care they pay for, although that does happen. It is much deeper than that. As a society we read the real worth of a good or an activity from the financial value placed on it. For people at work this means that pay and status are very closely related, with low-paid workers rarely garnering much respect, no matter how skilled or important their work is. For paid care workers it means that their status will always be a reflection of the way in which society thinks about women's traditional reproductive roles in the home. All the time that domestic labour is seen as inherently worthless and unskilled because women normally do it for free, those who are paid to do it will be considered in the same way.

The low status and low pay of domestic work and other forms of care work have created shortages of labour at precisely the same time as demand for help in the home has increased. The solution offered by government to these labour shortages is to import cheaper labour from abroad, as detailed in Chapter 2, rather than addressing the core issues, such as the unequal burdens of domestic labour between men and women and the shortages of collective care for both young children and the elderly. Thus the gross inequalities in our society, between rich and poor, men and women, are not addressed. Instead their effects are internationalized, passed on to a global workforce of poor, disenfranchised and often exploited women.

The increasingly neo-liberal, deregulated, slimmed-down, business-friendly climate has had a profound effect on how people organize their home lives as well as their work. It has exacerbated income inequalities, cut welfare spending, increased working hours and insecurity. All these things have fed into domestic employment. They have created households where people can afford to pay others for help and lifestyles that need to be maintained. They have placed other people in dire straits, with few opportunities except informal sector work, or domestic work in foreign countries. One positive change in the last 20 years has been women's increased participation in paid work, particularly in well-paid and professional jobs. However, while current trends in women's employment are a step forward from the sexist attitudes that have restricted women for so long, without other changes – for example, in men's behaviour at home, and employers' attitudes towards families – these new work habits have not made women's lives that much easier. For many families the extent to which changes in women's expectations have not been supported by changes elsewhere, becomes clear when they need childcare.

4 | Minding the gaps
The crisis in childcare

The failure of successive governments to respond to families' needs for childcare, and of employers to provide any really family-friendly employment, has resulted in a crisis of childcare which, for many families, can only be resolved by recourse to private arrangements. While more and more women work outside the home and work long hours in demanding jobs, there has been no corresponding increase in public provision of childcare: less than 2 per cent of children under 3 years old have access to subsidized care and less than 1 per cent of school age children receive subsidized care outside school hours. This chapter examines the care that is available for children of different ages and the relative costs and limitations of different arrangements. Many families struggle to negotiate the demands of childcare and work and enter into complex arrangements to manage these. Some better-off families are able to pay for private care, and private nurseries have grown to make up some of the shortfall left by the public sector. Out-of-school clubs for older children are also popular. However, the cost and inflexibility of these makes them unsuitable for some families and they are only available in practice to a small proportion of school children. An average au pair will be paid less than the cost of leaving two children in an after-school club for two hours a day and a nanny can cost less than full-time care for one child in a private nursery. In addition a nanny or au pair will provide more hours of care, more flexible care and might do the housework as well!

When my research led me to investigate the state of childcare provision in Britain I was shocked by what I found. I was stunned by the inadequacy of most arrangements, the inflexibility, the phenomenal expense and downright rarity of most forms of care. I couldn't believe that parents weren't standing on rooftops screaming about such an unworkable situation. Later I discovered that lots of people were screaming about it, and were starting to be listened to. Many others wanted to go out and scream but, as the saying goes, couldn't find a babysitter.

The National Childcare Strategy marks the first attempt by government to meet the country's childcare needs. It has delivered some good things but has much more to do. The National Childcare Strategy is part of a wider political philosophy that defines work as the only way out of poverty, rather than considering childcare as a right for all families. This means that its provision is aimed at helping people into work and overlooks the needs of unemployed families and those on average or above average incomes. Its focus is on providing care during the 'standard working day'. It does not focus on parents who work non-standard hours or aim to provide care while parents do anything other than work.

In 1998, when the government launched its childcare strategy, its aims were to 'ensure good quality, affordable childcare for children aged 0 to 14 in every neighbourhood'. The policy identified the variable quality of provision, the high cost of childcare and the lack of readily accessible childcare as failings of the existing system. However, five years later, in 2003, the average cost of childcare was at an all-time high of more than £6,650 a year and more than three-quarters of parents reported a lack of quality, affordable childcare in their area.[1] There is clearly still a crisis in childcare provision, a crisis that prevents many parents working, that reduces the flexibility of those who do work, and that underpins demand for flexible, private childcare in the home.

Childcare provision

Britain has a long tradition of high numbers of women working outside their homes and very low levels of government investment in childcare provision. Like many other Western countries the late twentieth century saw a privatization of many forms of care and a scaling down of the welfare state. Conservative and Labour governments alike had traditionally regarded childcare as the responsibility of individual parents. As Penelope Leach puts it: 'Outside the Nordic nations, where children's care is regarded as a joint responsibility of parents and the state, Western governments leave responsibility for children to their natural families as a matter of individualist *laissez-faire* principle – and economics.'[2] Ruth Fincher describes Britain as an extreme example of a country where government philosophy has left childcare to the market and resisted any intrusion 'for fear of reducing "efficiency" '.[3] In addition, Fincher reports that governments throughout the 1980s and 1990s supported the notion that children under 3 years old should be cared for full time by their mothers or their development would be harmed. As a result childcare provision has been left to non-government sectors and a philosophy of 'mother-like' care as best has been supported.

This section examines the main provisions of recent government policy on childcare and then reviews what childcare is available to children of different ages. It compares the costs, availability and flexibility of different forms of care to reveal the ways in which choices are extremely constrained for most parents. It shows that the current government approach still makes the employment of a nanny or au pair a logical, economic and perhaps inevitable option for parents who feel they have no other choice.

The National Childcare Strategy: affordable childcare?

Until the development of the National Childcare Strategy in 1998 local authorities were left to make provision as they saw fit. This led to extremely variable provision and an overall, minimal level of subsidized care. So that whereas only 2 per cent of children under 3 years old in the UK had access to subsidized childcare, 20 per cent of children in France had access to subsidized care, as did 85 per cent of children in Denmark. Two authors reporting on the paucity of childcare at that time commented that: 'The typical mother in the UK would have access to no childcare facilities other than those accidentally resulting from the school system.'[4] Within this, regional variations were huge. In the mid 1990s the number of registered day nursery places per 1,000 children under 5 ranged from 115.3 in Calderdale, West Yorkshire, to just 5.3 in Harrow, North London.[5] Since 1998 there has been some improvement in provision of childcare but there is still a huge gap between places available and the number of children who need them. The Daycare Trust, a national childcare charity that campaigns for high-quality, affordable childcare, calculates that there is one childcare place for every 6.7 children under 8 years old, and that whilst the number of places in day nurseries and out-of-school clubs has increased since the introduction of the National Childcare Strategy, the number of places with childminders, one of the most flexible and affordable forms of care, has fallen by 60,600.[6]

After five years of a national strategy there are still huge problems facing families who try to combine work with childrearing. There is not enough childcare available, that which is available is inflexible and does not fit with everyone's working patterns and most forms of childcare are still prohibitively expensive for most families. In fact, only 13 per cent of parents with dependent children can afford to use formal childcare services all the time, even if they cut back on everything else and do without a pension.[7] As the Daycare Trust concludes: 'For most parents there is no choice – childcare is either too expensive or simply not available.'[8]

One of the main ways in which the government has sought to meet childcare needs is by helping parents pay for privately provided childcare through the childcare element of Working Tax Credit. This is a credit given to parents who work over 16 hours a week. If living as a couple both parents must be in paid work or one parent must be in work and the other incapacitated. The credit is only given for registered or approved care and cannot be paid to relatives unless they are registered or approved – for example, as a childminder. Nannies are now covered by the scheme if they are inspected but they were not included in original proposals.

The maximum cost of childcare that can be claimed for is £135 per week for one child or £200 per week for two or more children. Parents are then paid a percentage of that cost based on their earnings. The maximum amount that is paid to any parent is 70 per cent of the cost. That would be £94.50 per week for one child or £140 per week for two children, which works out at an absolute maximum of £7,280 a year. This sounds like a sizeable benefit but it does only apply to the poorest working families. In order for two working parents to qualify for the maximum, they would have to have at least two children in childcare and have a gross income of £14,950 a year or less. The amount parents are entitled to declines as income rises and a family with two parents working and two children in childcare, paying £200 a week or more for care, that has a combined gross income of £34,500 would be entitled to only £36 per year towards childcare. A family on an average income with only one child in childcare would be unlikely to get any help at all.[9]

The tax credit works more as a benefit for the lowest paid than as a real help for all working families. But even for those on low incomes it is grossly inadequate and hardly likely to help parents into work. A family which is eligible for the highest rate of credit has an income barely more than half the average for the country, i.e. only just above the poverty line. However, this family would still have to contribute £60 per week in childcare costs, i.e. £3,120 a year, or more than 20 per cent of their gross income, in order to be eligible for the maximum tax credit because the credit only covers 70 per cent of costs. The family with an income just above average that would receive just £36 a year in tax credit would need to be paying over £10,000 a year for approved childcare to be eligible for this meagre help. Other problems include the fact that the maxima have not changed recently despite childcare costs rising at 7 per cent a year, more than twice the rate of inflation, and that real childcare costs are often well above the maxima set, particularly for families with more than one child needing care.[10] Few childcare providers do give a discount for siblings and even when they do it is unlikely to be more than 5–10 per cent of the cost. Childcare costs can be a particular problem for parents with twins or larger multiple births, and there is no allowance made for the very high childcare costs these parents can face.[11]

Very few parents, therefore, can afford to pay the whole cost of childcare, and government tax credits do not provide enough help for enough families. Yet there is also an inherent problem in trying to make childcare cheaper. The greatest component of the cost of formal childcare is wages for childcare workers. These make up about 60 per cent of costs in private nurseries and closer to 100 per cent of the costs of a childminder. This means there is no way of bringing childcare costs down without making wages lower, yet childcare workers are already very poorly paid, many earning only the minimum wage; even a nursery manager would earn only £13,000–15,000 a year for very long hours.[12] Because pay is so low, recruiting staff is a real problem for the sector. This affects one of the government's other main approaches to tackling the childcare crisis, that of creating more places for 3 and 4 year olds in local authority nursery schools and classes. The aim was to offer a place to all families that wanted one by April 2004, but problems with the recruitment and retention of staff persist.

Inadequacies in childcare mean that those on low wages leave the workforce while the well-off buy private help. This has the effect of polarizing families as those without work lose money, skills, experience and the ability to re-enter work. The better-off who have stayed in work become more flexible, can work harder, for longer hours and become still better off.

'Would you like a second mortgage with that babygro?' Paying the price for pre-school care

For most families the maximum amount of childcare is needed for pre-school children, in the UK before they reach 4 or 5 years old. However, since care for children under 2 tends to be the most expensive, working parents find themselves having to pay for the largest number of hours of care just at the point when it is most expensive. Many parents returning to work after starting a family discover that they are paying more for childcare than for housing and food. There are almost no state facilities for children under 3 years old and the National Childcare Strategy has not directly provided for the needs of this group, so the options for most parents looking for full-time, or part-time care are a childminder, a place in a private nursery or a nanny at home.

Childminders provide care in their own homes. They are normally women who have young children themselves and they have to be registered with the local authority and inspected by OFSTED (the Office for Standards in Education). The local authority regulates how many children in each age group a childminder can take and inspects the childminder's home on a yearly basis. Childminders have long been an important source of childcare in Britain. They tend to be located close to the families of the children that they care for and can often offer flexible, affordable care for just the hours parents need. There are over 72,000 registered childminders in Britain providing care for over 300,000 children.[13] The typical cost of a full-time place with a childminder for a child under two is £118 per week. This varies between £141 per week in eastern England and £93 per week in the north-west, with London, the south-east and the east being substantially more expensive than other parts of England.[14]

Many parents favour childminders because they provide care in a 'family' atmosphere, often alongside the minder's own children. They can also provide great continuity of care, taking children full time when they are very young and then caring for them outside school hours as they get older. Because childminders will generally care for more than one child at a time, their rates are lower than a dedicated nanny and this makes them affordable to a much larger number of families. However, the costs for parents of using a childminder increase dramatically if they have more than one child that needs childcare. As minders charge per child, the cost of having two children cared for full time by a minder is more than many women earn and close to the cost of employing a nanny. Childminders do offer some flexibility in terms of the hours they cover, and children can normally be dropped off before work and picked up afterwards. However, there are going to be limits to their flexibility in terms of late evenings or weekends, which makes them less useful to some parents. The number of childminders has also decreased recently[15] and in some areas there are severe shortages of childminders and parents find it impossible to get a childminder in a location that allows them to co-ordinate dropping off children and travelling to work on time.

In contrast provision in private nurseries has increased dramatically, with the private daycare sector valued at £2.15 billion in May 2003 and providing care for 400,000 children, that is five times the size it was at the beginning of the 1990s.[16] The cost of private nurseries has also been increasing; in 2004 in London the cost of a nursery place increased by 17 per cent. The average cost of a full-time place for a child under 2 is £141 per week. However in some areas costs are much higher and parents in inner London typically pay £197 per week, over £10,244 per year.[17]

Private nurseries are also inspected and regulated by OFSTED, who consider the levels of staffing and the educational benefits of activities made available to children. Some nurseries provide excellent facilities and a stimulating and caring environment, supervised by qualified and experienced staff. Just as some parents specifically choose childminders because the care they provide is 'mother-like', others favour the socializing and educational approach of a nursery. Private nurseries are generally open for longer hours than a school, often from 7.30 or 8.00 am until 6.00 pm, and for more weeks of the year. This makes them useful to more families working full time and does allow some leeway for travel at the beginning and end of the working day. However, even expensive private nurseries do not offer a suitable solution for parents who work non-standard hours, shifts or have their hours varied with little notice. The cost of full-time nursery care is clearly a barrier for many families too. With the average annual pay of a woman working full time being £6,700 less than for a man[18] there are large numbers of families who simply would not see £7,332 per year as feasible. There are even fewer parents who would be able to afford the cost of two children needing full-time care and again, those who could afford it might find it cheaper and more convenient to employ a nanny.

Leticia Youngman, a new mother I interviewed in North London, had started planning childcare before her daughter was born. She wanted to stay at home full time for at least the first six months after giving birth and then to return to work part time, two or three days a week. She said she would actually have liked a longer break, at least a year, but feared that her work environment was too competitive and a long absence would harm her reputation at work and her career. When she first started looking for childcare Leticia had assumed she would find a nursery place or childminder in her local area. She got a list of registered childminders from her local authority and asked friends for advice and recommendations about other forms of care. Once she knew when she would be going back to work she started looking in earnest and began with the nurseries. There were only two that she could get to easily but neither of these was open long enough for her or her partner to collect their daughter after work. A possible solution was to rely on her mother to collect her daughter in the evenings but Leticia was reluctant to depend on an arrangement that put such a burden on her increasingly frail mother. Next she turned to her list of childminders and began by phoning those closest to her house. As she worked down the list she discovered there was not a single one with a space for a child under 2 years old.

Leticia explained that she had been absolutely stunned and very upset when she realized that there was no childcare available for her daughter. She had assumed that living in a large city and being able to afford to pay, she would be able to find something, even if it meant travelling some distance. The problems she faced with childcare compounded her frustration with having to return to work before she really wanted to and she said she briefly considered a more permanent withdrawal from the workforce, despite having spent years building her career. In the end a friend put her in touch with someone else who worked part time and had a nanny. Leticia was able to arrange a share so that the nanny worked for her two days a week and for her original employer on the other three and so Leticia was able to go back to work. She described the situation as very far from ideal. She had always wanted her daughter to be in a more social form of care, able to be with other children. She also confessed that she had always scorned 'the type of women who have nannies' and was appalled to find she had become one.

Like so many women, Leticia was caught between a model of working life that does not recognize the burdens placed on women in the home, and a childcare system that does not really expect new mothers to work. Leticia and her partner had enough money to pay for a nanny to solve this conundrum, but most other parents would not. Leticia was also highly motivated to return to work because of her commitment to her career and the long-term costs a period away from work would bring in terms of lost promotions and future earnings. Many women working in less well-paid or competitive environments might well have decided to leave work altogether.

Nursery schools a help?

As children get a bit older the cost of care falls slightly and the amount of care they need can be reduced if they have access to a place in a nursery provided by the local authority. The National Childcare Strategy concentrated greatest resources on 3 and 4 year olds, and particularly on absorbing them into the education system. This began with the guarantee of a free 'early education' place for every 3 and 4 year old by April 2004. Since this target has been met greater attention is being paid to younger and older children through the 'Sure Start' programme.[19] This means that for parents of 3 and 4 year olds there is now more help from the state but there are still problems with the way this childcare is organized.

The expansion of local authority places for young children has been made possible by many schools taking 4 year olds into reception classes and government figures show that, in 2000, 29 per cent of all 3 and 4 year olds were actually in infant classes in primary schools rather than specific nursery classes. This compares with 30 per cent in nursery classes in primary schools and nursery schools, and another 30 per cent in places provided by the private and voluntary sectors.[20] In other words, the government was able to meet its early targets so quickly by effectively extending the school starting age downwards rather than by massive new provision of nursery schools and classes.

There has been a considerable expansion of nursery provision and £226 million was invested in nursery places for 3 year olds in 2001–2.[21] Nursery schools and classes can provide an excellent environment for children and give them foundations for getting the most out of the education system and life after that. However, they don't provide a great childcare solution for working parents because of the short hours they are open. Nursery places may be for only half a day and only for 40 weeks per year, resulting in an average of 525 hours of provision per place per year. By comparison a Danish childcare place would provide 1,500 hours per year.[22] The outcome of this approach is that families are forced to make other arrangements. These might include opting for a private nursery which is open longer hours, even though this would be much more expensive, employing a childminder to take and/or collect children from nursery to extend the time covered, or employing a nanny or au pair. For families with more than one young child the latter options can be the cheapest and the fact that government-provided nursery care for 3 year olds is for relatively short hours can be the trigger that means that a family chooses to have a nanny rather than pay for a private nursery or childminder for a baby and a childminder to cover the gaps for a child at nursery.

Care for school age children

Similar problems occur for parents of school age children, who need fewer hours of care than the very young but still need enough care to make working difficult for parents. Government strategy has been to support the increase in the number of places available in out-of-school clubs. These are normally based in school buildings or very near by and provide care for children for an hour or two after school and sometimes for a short time in the morning too. Many out-of-school clubs also provide some kind of care during school holidays. However, they are not necessarily run by schools, and while some are well subsidized they charge a fee per child per hour or session. The Daycare Trust estimates that the number of out-of-school clubs grew from just 350 in the early 1990s to almost 5,000 by the end of the decade, providing places for over 150,000 children. About 42 per cent of schemes in England and Wales are operated by the voluntary sector, 16 per cent by schools, and the rest by private or community businesses. However, even this increased provision only provides places for about 3–4 per cent of primary school age children in England, and in Wales and Northern Ireland the proportion is even lower. Clubs tend to be concentrated in urban areas and in affluent areas where parents are more able to pay.[23] There is also very little provision for children at secondary school. While these children may need less 'care' than younger ones, they may well need supported activities in the times that their parents are not available. The Daycare Trust argues that the out-of-school needs of children in the 10–14 age group need to be explicitly considered in order to reduce their involvement in crime, drug-taking, drinking and to improve their health, educational attainment and general wellbeing.[24]

Out-of-school clubs are set to continue their expansion but will still not provide a suitable solution for many working parents. One barrier is their lack of flexibility, providing care for set hours each day which need to be booked in advance. For parents who need childcare after 5.30 or 6.00 pm out-of-school clubs do not work. Nor do they work for parents whose hours change at short notice, or who work at weekends. The cost can also be prohibitive. Typically an after-school club would charge about £5 per evening per child (often more if children are left past 5.00 pm). Similar amounts are charged for morning sessions by clubs where those are provided. The Daycare Trust found that the typical cost of an after-school club was £34 for 15 hours a week.[25] Thirty-four pounds per week compares well with other forms of care, but for a parent using more hours, or with two (or more) children, the cost can be closer to £100 per week, that is £4,000 a year just to cover term weeks. Holiday schemes are an additional, higher charge. By comparison an au pair is paid just £45 per week for 25 hours of work and two evenings babysitting – substantially less than putting two children in an out-of-school club for one hour each evening and less than a lot of people pay for one child in an out-of-school club and a cleaner for an afternoon each week. Of course, au pairs have to be housed somewhere and they must be fed but in return they do ironing, childcare, cleaning and myriad other things for ridiculously low pay.

Parents whom I interviewed who had children of school age had often imagined that their childcare arrangements would be solved as their children got older, only to find them more complicated and just as intractable as before. Those that solved the conundrum and 'filled the gaps' by employing an au pair were generally quite ambivalent about this choice and looked forward longingly to the day their children would be old enough to look after themselves. As one mother put it: 'I'm just really looking forward to when we can get the house back.' This group of 'au parents' saw themselves as forced into taking on an au pair because of the problems with all other childcare options.

One family I interviewed, the Campbells, typified this situation. Marion and Simon Campbell had three children and had employed au pairs for about three years when I talked to them. They had moved to London from the Midlands, before having children, to access better jobs. Both had jobs that they enjoyed and were proud of. When they first had children Marion started a business and began to work from home, briefly employing a part-time nanny. When the children went to school Marion found working from home still seemed to be a good solution, but when their housing costs went up Marion decided the business did not make enough money and looked for a more regular income by going back out to work. The Campbells were then faced with having to get three children to two different schools in the morning and getting them back home in the evening and cared for until one of their parents returned later on. One of the children's schools had an after-school club, which looked like a potential solution, but it would not take the children who attended the other school. It was also not open late enough to give any flexibility and would have meant one or other parent leaving meetings early or facing fines from the club for collecting children late. The Campbells decided that a live-in au pair was the only solution to their problems. As Simon Campbell explained:

> . . . both people were essentially going to be away from home from nine o'clock in the morning until six o'clock, seven o'clock or whenever, meetings or whatever allowing. If you've got three children, unless you've got an extended family which is very close, where you've got either mother-in-law or grandparents or somebody else who can look after the children during the day, you have no choice but actually to employ someone.

The Campbells felt that they had explored all the existing options and that there was no other source of care available to them. The only alternative was for one of them to reduce the hours they worked in order to fill the gaps before and after school themselves. Marion would probably have considered doing this but shorter hours, to fit the school day, were not on offer to her – despite the fact that she worked for a local authority co-ordinating the provision of childcare services.

The cost, inflexibility and rarity of formal childcare mean that ultimately very few families are able to rely on these arrangements and that most families need to find different ways to solve their childcare problems. For people who cannot make informal arrangements outside the market, such as relying on a relative or neighbour to help out, the options are to cut back on their own participation in work or to pay someone to come in to look after their children. Either way, few families see these as choices, freely made, more as the only options available. Interviews I carried out with parents employing both nannies and au pairs revealed that some of them had become employers reluctantly after trying other childcare arrangements or after struggling to find other sources of care for young children in their local area. The realities of both the labour market and childcare provision mean that it is difficult for most families to combine work with childrearing. In the following chapters I will explore the domestic arrangements of a range of households that employ help. The majority of these people have not been forced into their current arrangements, though some parents do feel that they have no alternative but to employ private help. Alternatives to social childcare are also becoming increasingly problematic and causing an increasing division between those families who pay for private help and those who withdraw from participation in paid work.

Keeping it in the family

Families who cannot afford private domestic help, but for whom the extant childcare is still inadequate, often turn to relatives to fill the gaps. In fact, grandmothers are the most important source of childcare, after parents, for children of all ages.[26] However, demographic trends and increased mobility mean that family members are less often able to help out than they may have been in the past.

The importance of relatives' help in providing childcare can hardly be underestimated. Government statistics show that for families where both or the only parent works there is a strong reliance on family members: 18 per cent of all pre-school children are cared for by a relative and a similar proportion of children aged 4–14 years are cared for by a relative during term time. In the school holidays even more families rely on their relatives to help.[27] Family members are also a particularly important source of care for families that work non-standard hours. The inflexible organization of most formal childcare means that relatives and friends are really the only source of care available to many families who cannot afford a nanny or au pair. Relatives, and in particular children's grandmothers, therefore play an extremely important part in facilitating parents' work and with it their wider participation in society.

Unfortunately, changes in the way we live and work will make it increasingly difficult for families to make these kinds of arrangements in the future. Grandparents and other relatives are less likely to live near by as people become more mobile, moving around the country to look for work or follow employers. This is particularly an issue in cities like London that have many young families who have moved in from other parts of the country or from other parts of the world. Grandmothers are also less likely to be available to look after children because they may be working themselves or have other caring responsibilities. Grandmothers are more likely to be working outside the home now than in previous generations. The trend in women's increased employment has not passed older women by and even women who did not work when they were younger are now joining the workforce. Indeed, some employers, such as the large supermarkets, have targeted women near retirement age as reliable but pliable employees. Perhaps more depressing than this is the fact that women often have to care for their own elderly parents once their children are grown up.

The ageing population means that there are more people who need a measure of care and more very old people who need large amounts of care. This work overwhelmingly falls to female family members who then find that demands are being made on them from all sides. Women in their 50s and 60s are increasingly caring for older and younger generations of the family at the same time.

The new repertoires of care

One outcome of the complexities and inadequacies of the childcare system is that families develop sophisticated 'repertoires of care'[28] using a range of different sources of care on different days of the week or weeks of the year. Figures show that 15 per cent of pre-school children use more than one type of care and 6 per cent of school age children use more than one type of care during term time.[29] However, these figures can disguise the complexities of arrangements that parents have to make to get their children from one type of care to another as well as between home, school and anywhere else they need to be. It is not unusual to find a child who is taken to school by a neighbour on a couple of days each week, goes to an after-school club for an hour every day and is then collected by a minder on three of those days, collected by a parent on the other days to be and taken to an activity such as sport or drama from which their other parent will then collect them. With more than one child, particularly if the children are in different schools and taking part in different activities, the patterns can become extremely complicated and just remembering their details each day is a labour in itself.

For many parents reciprocal and informal arrangements with friends and neighbours can be a lifeline, but the complexities of some repertoires holds its own problems. Not only is arranging and remembering so many separate parts difficult – they are also delicate houses of cards, and the slightest problem in one part of the arrangement can have a knock-on effect on all the other bits. In situations like this there is rarely any slack in the system and the illness of a child, parent or childcare professional can cause havoc. Working parents can end up missing work and can suffer great anxiety because of the precariousness of their childcare arrangements. This anxiety can be yet another reason to buy in private help, for those who can afford it, but for those who can't it might be yet another reason to give up the battle and to stop trying to combine work and childcare.

Withdrawing from the workforce

And giving up the battle is just what many women do. While it is true that more women than ever are participating in paid work outside the home, there are others who are not able to work purely because they cannot find acceptable childcare. This is a huge problem not just for those families but also for society more generally. The result of the inflexibility and expense of most childcare options is that for many families it is just not worthwhile using childcare outside the home. It is too expensive, inflexible, distant or just plain rare, to be a solution.

For those on the lowest pay the decision to give up work is likely to be the most obvious. Even with the childcare element of Working Tax Credit, families still have to find 30 per cent of the cost of most forms of childcare and this can be more than many can afford. Low-paid work is also increasingly associated with flexible or non-standard hours that can make finding childcare virtually impossible. The Daycare Trust found that 28 per cent of unemployed mothers in couples said that they were not working because they could not find work that had suitable hours. They also found that 41 per cent of lone parents faced the same problem.[30] Women who are low paid and low skilled are least likely to return to work after having children and they can then face barriers if they later do want to go back to work. Skills can become out of date and women can lose their confidence once they have left the workforce. The result is that families are more likely to face poverty and that pressures on a partner who is working to increase their hours grow, causing additional strains within the family.

Women who earn a bit more, and particularly those who are committed to a career, are more likely to try to balance the demands of home and work, but still many relatively well-paid and highly educated women find this impossible. In fact fewer mothers are in full-time employment 10 years after the birth of their first baby than had been within 12 months of that birth. And only 1 in 10 women are able to maintain full-time, continuous employment during the first 11 years after starting a family.[31] Of course, not all mothers want to stay in full-time employment but many who do find it impossible because of the difficulties of finding affordable childcare. The government admits that four out of five parents who are out of work would work if they could access childcare.[32]

This is a particularly important issue because parental employment is the central plank of the government's anti-poverty and anti-social exclusion strategy. The theory is that working allows people to gain an income to provide resources and to engage with networks that alleviate social exclusion. The government has specifically emphasized the importance of employment for parents, including lone parents, as a way of reducing child poverty and of reducing what are called the 'lifecycle effects' of poverty, i.e. the ways that children raised in poverty or by unemployed parents are least likely to achieve at school and are most likely to become unemployed adults.[33] This policy is in contrast to previous governments' approaches, which have stressed the importance of care by mothers to early child development and have done little to enhance childcare provision or to push lone parents out to work. Poverty reduction has been approached through trying to support two-parent families – particularly married couples – in a traditional male breadwinner model and by encouraging work, even at very low levels of pay, for everyone except mothers. The current employment-focused strategy may seem like a step forward from this, but without adequate, accessible childcare it will only repeat past mistakes and create a more polarized society divided between those able to access work and those trapped in unemployment.

Inadequate childcare also represents a cost to the economy if parents are unable to work. The skills, experience and education that they have are 'wasted' in economic terms when parents stay at home to look after their children – although both parents and children might find that time very far from a waste. As far as business is concerned the large numbers of women who find it impossible to re-enter the workforce after having children represent a pool of talent that is unavailable because of childcare problems. However, few employers act to ameliorate these difficulties or to share the costs of childcare. Only about one in ten working parents get any help with childcare from employers.[34] Many employers have also been reluctant to support or implement practices designed to help parents combine work and childcare, such as term-time working or other flexible patterns. They see these as too expensive, and fail to estimate the costs that already exist because so many parents are kept out of the workforce.

In addition to parents who withdraw from the workforce altogether there are many others who reduce the hours they work or who change to less demanding work, and for many people this is to fit in with the childcare that is available or because employers are uninterested in working around parents' needs. While part-time work may seem to offer a good balance between home and the workplace it is often a far from ideal solution because part-time workers tend to be restricted to low-wage and low-status work. Those who do try to negotiate part-time work in a more professional environment find it difficult to be taken seriously and are considered to lack commitment. As a result they are often not considered for promotion. As Barbara Castle said, in 1974: 'Part-time workers are second-class citizens entitled to third-class benefits.'[35] In the United States the institution of the 'mommy track' is recognized. This gives women flexibility at work but no progression through the hierarchy. The 'mommy track' was first proposed by Felice Schwartz in an article in the *Harvard Business Review* in 1987. She suggested that professional women who are mothers could be put on a permanently lower 'non-career dominant' track at work, which effectively institutionalizes the assumption that working mothers are not really committed to their jobs.[36]

What do you get in the 'Gucci Zone of Nannies'[37]: Paying for private care in your home

It seems that employing a nanny or au pair is a cost-effective solution for many families in need of childcare (particularly if they have more than one young child) and perhaps the only possible option for some people working non-standard hours who do not have family or friends to fill the gaps. So what do parents who take this route actually get for their money?

Nannies

Nannies are normally trained and qualified childcarers who are competent to be sole carers to babies as well as older children. Nannies can live out or in, are paid anything from minimum wage to over £25,000 a year and are normally young women who do not yet have children themselves. Live-in nannies tend to earn less but also tend to be less experienced, as often nannies aim to live out when they can command a high enough salary to cover their own housing costs, something that comes with age and experience. In general, nannies will provide for all a child's needs during the working day. They may arrive, or begin duty, at breakfast time, give the children breakfast, get them washed and dressed. Depending on the ages of the children being cared for they might take them to planned activities such as mother and toddler groups, swimming, music lessons, etc. They cook lunch and often tea for the children and hand over when parents return from work or sometimes after parents have eaten supper if they live in. It can all make for a very long day for the nanny and timings will be adjusted to suit the parents' working patterns. It is quite a different situation from that of parents trying to co-ordinate moving their children between three different forms of care every day just to cover their work hours.

In theory nannies are meant to be childcare professionals who are responsible for providing a caring and stimulating environment for their charges. This would include taking care of everything relating to the children, like washing their clothes and tidying away their toys, but it is not really meant to include too much other housework. In practice many families want a 'nanny/housekeeper' and will turn their nanny into a housekeeper quite readily. Many nannies are expected to do much of the housework, to do washing for all the family, run errands, wait for deliveries and even cook the family meals. Those who live in are also expected to babysit in the evenings and many are expected to get up in the night if they are caring for a small baby. In recent years there has been a relative shortage of qualified nannies and this 'sellers' market' has tended to push up wages.[38] This has allowed more nannies to live out and others to escape the most demanding employers, so conditions do seem to have improved. However, a quick look at the advertisements in *The Lady* magazine soon reveals many employers wanting nannies who will live in, work weekends, work 11-hour shifts and babysit in the evenings.

Those who can pay top dollar can employ a 'Norlander' – a nanny who has trained at Norland College. This college was established in 1892 as the first real training college for nannies and is thriving to this day despite course fees of £24,000. Norlanders were famous for their stiff uniforms of brown dresses, hats and white gloves that were still a feature in the late 1990s. Today the college takes a slightly more relaxed view but still has a strong reputation and Norlanders are favoured by many parents.[39]

Au pairs

Au pair employers get a different kind of help. Au pairs are not trained and are not required to have any experience of working with children or carrying out housework. They are not meant be the sole carers for babies or to work for more than 25 hours a week. They are expected to do some childcare and also do housework and they can be asked to babysit for two evenings a week in addition to their other duties. Families with school age children can use an au pair to fill the gap between the end of the school day and when parents return home. Many au pairs will take children to afterschool activities, cook their tea or help with homework. Au pairs can also provide appropriate care for younger children when one parent works part time. In addition au pairs will do cleaning and ironing and because they live in they can be called upon at short notice if plans change or more babysitting is needed. Most au pairs seem to work many more hours than Home Office guidance suggests and in fact do large amounts of housework, childcare and babysitting. In effect, au pair employers may get full-time help with childcare and housework, and even home maintenance and gardening, all for a fraction of the cost of a nanny, or even a place in a private nursery.

Having private help means that everything is easier. Worries are lessened and planning becomes simpler. You may still need to think about whether little Henry has his PE kit, but someone else has probably washed it and packed it, made his lunch and will take him to school safely. A nanny or au pair is not just an extra pair of hands to do whatever you want them to do: they are also another person to share the worry, a service no socialized form of care will ever be able to provide. However, what you get when you enter the nanny zone is not just a supply of childcare in the hours you identify, or a cheap source of cleaning, it is the control of another person's labour and a relationship that can be delicate and intimate. For many parents it is these elements of nanny or au pair employment that are important in their decision to employ or not employ. Some families would run a mile from the hierarchical relationship that employing domestic help suggests, while others are attracted to the status and increased leisure that result from having someone else to take on household tasks.

5 | The new 'upstairs, downstairs'

The majority of media coverage that has been given to the growth in domestic employment in contemporary Britain has focused on nanny employment and the fears that working parents have about leaving their children with a stranger all day. However, large numbers of domestic workers are employed for reasons other than to allow parents to work. Domestic workers are employed to enhance the standard of living of their employers. They create leisure, ensure comfortable surroundings and display status. Some are employed in very formal, multi-staff households that we think of as having died out long ago but many others are employed by the 'relaxed rich' middle class, who would not dream of employing a butler, but neither would they dream of doing their own cleaning.

This chapter explores forms of domestic help that are not taken on to allow busy parents to work but that provide status, luxury and increased leisure. It looks first at the domestic arrangements of the most wealthy: at the employment of butlers, valets, cooks and other formal domestic staff. It then turns to the habits of the less formal, but still wealthy, middle class, such as the employment of nannies by women who do not work and the increasing use of paid cleaners. It also examines the cruelty that some workers face at the hands of their privileged employers.

There are relatively small numbers of formal multi-staff households where newspapers are ironed and everyone is in uniform, but the numbers are still larger than you would think. My discussions with agencies that place 'top end' domestic workers suggested that there are perhaps 3,000 butlers in Britain, and a similar number of dedicated chauffeurs. There are probably more than twice this number of formal housekeepers and cooks and a larger number still of 'couples' – married people who work as domestic staff together with the woman usually acting as cook and housekeeper and the man as butler, gardener and handyman. There are small numbers of under-butlers, footmen and valets and even some people whose job titles are 'parlour maid' and 'lady's maid'. Formal households also employ nannies when there are children and can have part-time, live-out cleaners alongside their full-time staff. They may also employ au pairs to supplement trained staff. All in all this is not a huge sector, but there could be over 10,000 people employed in formal households in Britain.

As well as the thoroughly formal, 'top end' households, there are surprisingly large numbers of less starchy families who employ some help (and sometimes quite a lot) in order to preserve their lifestyle and status rather than to facilitate work outside the home. These families will not employ butlers or valets but they may have full-time housekeepers, cooks, nannies or au pairs (even though one parent is at home), gardeners and lots of hours of a cleaner's time. These households range from the very rich, who have lots of staff but don't want them in uniform, to more middle-class families and single people who create leisure time and an easier life by paying for help.

The distinction between formal and informal households can be a bit hazy. Formal households would normally expect staff to wear uniforms when appropriate, address employers by their titles and last names and never to think of themselves as part of the family. By less formal households we do not mean ones that employ staff in the informal sector i.e. cash in hand, but rather households that attempt to be more relaxed in the ways they are organized. They would not expect staff to wear uniforms, for example, they may be on first name terms and they will tend to employ people to do different types of domestic work more frequently than do their more formal counterparts. The distinction between formal and less formal households is a useful one for thinking about the types of job that exist and the ways in which domestic workers are treated by different employers. It is also a distinction that is used by agencies placing staff in order to identify the 'right' kind of domestic worker for a particular job.

A group of domestic workers which may fall into either of these categories is the overseas domestic worker. These people come to Britain with their employers. Overseas domestic workers always live in and often work as housekeeper, cook and nanny all rolled into one. The visa status of these workers has made them vulnerable to abuse by employers and their situation reveals what can happen to workers who are isolated within their employers' homes and overlooked by the law. The ways in which they are treated raise awkward questions about why powerful people with plenty of money might be so cruel to workers who are impoverished and dependent upon them. The relationship between the work of domestic workers and the status of their employers perhaps offers some clues as to their treatment. It also raises some difficult questions about status, housework and domestic workers more broadly.

Butlers, valets and maids: the organization of formal households

Formal, multi-staff households are the 'elite' of domestic employers. They employ more staff, with higher levels of skill and better levels of pay than others. These are the households that seem to have changed least from the 'upstairs, downstairs' picture of centuries past. They tend to include jobs with the titles we know from novels, talk about domestic 'service' and tend to be located in some of the same houses that were great employers in the past. However, in all sorts of ways these jobs have changed dramatically and the pay and working conditions of elite domestic workers have much less in common with those of Victorian times than the conditions of domestic workers in smaller 'friendlier' households. Despite this, there is a strong historical influence that shapes the jobs done in formal households and who does them.

The historical legacy

The historical legacy of formal households is manifested in the types of domestic jobs that exist and in who is considered suitable to take on those jobs. Before the twentieth century the large country house or town residence had a staff that was organized into a strict hierarchy, with each member responsible for specific tasks within specific spaces. There were divisions between indoor and outdoor servants. Outdoor servants tended the gardens and stables and, before the industrial revolution, would have produced a wide variety of goods for the household such as linen, food and soap. Indeed, food production remained important on country estates until the middle of the twentieth century. Indoor servants cleaned, did laundry, processed foods, cooked and waited on the family. Within the 'indoor' servants group there were also upstairs and downstairs servants. The downstairs servants were responsible for kitchen duties and heavy cleaning while upstairs servants cleaned the spaces the family used and interacted with them directly. At the top of the hierarchy were body servants – such as ladies' maids and valets – who worked for individual members of the family, and the household managers – housekeepers, butlers and stewards.

The larger a household became the more complex its hierarchy was. A household with four housemaids did not have four maids of equal standing who did the same tasks but a first housemaid, a second housemaid, a third housemaid and a fourth housemaid. The fourth housemaid would have the largest share of the most unpleasant tasks and the first housemaid would have more of a supervisory role. Pamela Sambrook, in her study of the country house servant, gives the example of a large country house in West Sussex, which in 1872 was employing five laundrymaids. They were paid £25, £19, £17, £14 and £12 a year.[1] Servants at the bottom of the hierarchy waited on those at the top and worked the longest and least sociable hours.[2] In smaller and less well-off households the hierarchy became simpler and each servant was responsible for a greater range of tasks, until in lower middle-class and some working-class houses there was a single 'maid of all work'.

This pattern of organization has echoes in the formal households of today. Many of the job titles survive, as does the greater differentiation between jobs as the domestic staff becomes larger. There may not be the extremely nuanced hierarchy of former times but the largest households do keep some of the historical distinctions. The most extreme examples of this can perhaps be found in the royal palaces. Ryan Parry a *Daily Mirror* journalist who took as job as a footman at Buckingham Palace, reported:

> One weekend I joined another footman, two kitchen porters, two chefs, two silver pantry under-butlers, a page and a coffee-room maid – just to tend to the Queen. The maid waited two-and-a-half hours to pick up a pot of coffee from a hot plate and pour it into a silver jug. She then handed it to me. My role was to take the tray 20 metres to the page's vestibule and hand it to the page, who then carried it another eight metres to the Queen in her dining room.[3]

Of course, there are very few households with even a fraction of the staff that Buckingham Palace has, but the royal palaces do act as a model for the largest formal houses in the country.

One of the most important historical legacies is the gendered division of labour within domestic employment. The tax of 1777 made it more expensive to employ men than women as domestic servants. This had the effect of drastically reducing the overall numbers of men employed, of making firm delineations between farm and related workers, who were not taxed, and domestic servants who were, and of making the expensive male servants a status symbol to be shown publicly whenever possible. This last element obviously decided which work was done by male and female servants. Male servants appeared in public, opening doors, waiting at table, travelling on the coach when the family moved around. Footmen were the most ostentatious of these male servant status symbols. They were publicly displayed outside houses and coaches, dressed in expensive liveries designed to show off their employer's wealth. They followed women on walks and shopping trips, walking a few paces behind and carrying their packages. Tall men were particularly selected for this role and only men of above average height could aspire to be footmen. The 'better' the position the taller the footman had to be. Charles Booth, in his *Life and Labour of the People of London*, recorded that there was a widespread practice of paying footmen by height in the 1890s. A first footman of 5 feet 6 inches was paid up to £30 per year whilst one over 5 feet 10 inches was paid from £32 to £40 per annum.[4] Footmen with noticeable calf muscles were also favoured. One footman seeking work in 1850 advertised himself as 'tall, handsome, with broad shoulders and extensive calves'.[5] The logic underlying this preference for tall, strong men was not that footmen had a protective role or were needed to do heavy work. It was quite the opposite: footmen were for display and the better the physique of a man not used for productive labour the greater the waste and therefore the greater the social status of his employer.

Female servants were schooled to be as invisible as possible, particularly when they were carrying out their cleaning duties. Large houses were designed with intricate systems of passages, extra servants' staircases and invisible doors so that maids could move around the house without being seen by the family. A precise daily timetabling of tasks existed so that housemaids could clean rooms the moment the family stopped using them. So when the family went to breakfast, bedrooms were cleaned, when the bell went for dinner the drawing room could be cleaned. Maids were taught to be 'thoroughly unseen and unheard'. If a member of the family did appear unexpectedly while they were cleaning the maid was expected to dash away and hide. At least one employer, Lord Crewe of Crewe Hall in Cheshire, gave strict orders that any housemaid seen by his visitors would be instantly dismissed. A visitor to the hall remarked that he was puzzled to see a host of maids in the family chapel but only a flash of black dress disappearing around a corner at other times.[6] These practices continue to the present day in terms of the roles men and women take in formal houses. The most prestigious, visible and highly paid jobs are still done by men while the vast majority of domestic labour is carried out by women. A male butler is still a domestic status symbol of the highest order.

'The professionals': staff for formal households

While in the past all young women from poor families could expect to go into service, today securing a position in a large formal house can actually be very difficult. These domestic jobs are highly skilled and highly desirable, they require technical expertise, organizational skills and a particular personality. The best domestic jobs go to people with training, lots of experience and excellent references. Running a large house, cooking for dinner parties and looking after antique furniture are quite different from doing your own housework at home. The best-paid domestic workers work their way up through hierarchies, learning on the way.

Everyone is aware that the British royal family maintains formal households replete with footmen, ladies' maids and valets. We have seen television pictures of royal banquet rooms filled with liveried footmen and we have seen royal coaches driven by uniformed coachmen as if from a bygone time. The royal palaces play an important role within the formal domestic employment sector in Britain. They create employment for large numbers of domestic workers and act as an effective training ground for staff. A period working in the royal palaces is seen by some as a necessary prerequisite for employment in another formal household. The palaces provide an environment in which domestic workers can learn formal duties and behaviour and work within a complex hierarchy of staff. There are very few other households that are large enough to do this and many employers, therefore, like to take on staff who have worked in the palaces for at least a little while. Compared to other similar jobs, working in the royal palaces is poorly paid and living conditions are cramped. In 2003, when the journalist Ryan Parry worked as a footman at Buckingham Palace, he lived in a small room, sharing toilets and bathrooms with other staff. He was paid £11,811 a year, which was reduced to £9,338 after living costs were deducted.[7]

There are not many other households that have such a large staff but there are still thousands of formal domestic workers employed in contemporary Britain. Probably the most important positions numerically are housekeepers, cooks and couples. The housekeeper/cook is the favoured all-rounder for rich middle-and upper-class families, responsible for the complete running of the house and for cooking meals with perhaps a little help from a part-time live-out cleaner. Other households might employ just a housekeeper, who does less cooking or is expected to cook to a less impressive standard, whilst better-off households might employ a dedicated cook, able to cater for lavish dinner parties and other entertaining. Cooks and housekeepers earn £300–400 per week plus room and board. Housing can be a cottage or lodge on a country estate or a self-contained flat 'in town'. Some employers tolerate partners and children but many do not, particularly if children are young and might interfere with their staff's time.

Cooks and housekeepers

Cooks can be formally trained or have learnt to cater for large and extravagant meals through experience. Housekeepers are rarely trained but learn the necessary skills on the job, working their way up from smaller or less formal houses to larger ones, or from assistant housekeeper posts to being in charge. The skills involved are not as straightforward as it might seem – a large country house full of priceless antiques can need very specialist care and employers can have very exacting standards. One housekeeper I spoke to told of a job she had had in a large country house. The house was furnished with antiques that had to be meticulously cleaned using specialist techniques and a very delicate touch. The hall and reception rooms were carpeted with a luxurious deep pile carpet and all had to be vacuumed every day. The owners liked to see the effect when all the pile on the carpet went in the same direction so the housekeeper had to find a way to vacuum this very large area, finishing it all in the same direction without treading on a spot she had already done.

Many of the people doing this work in Britain are migrants from other countries; housekeepers and cooks are often women from Portugal, Spain and the Philippines. Their concentration in the sector is a legacy of earlier immigration policies that reserved work permits for domestic jobs for women from specific countries (see Chapter 2). Over time people from a particular country get a reputation as being suited to a particular post and the pattern of a nationality-determined job market becomes quite fixed. Employers tend to want to hire domestic workers who are like those they have found successful in the past. A worker's nationality or ethnicity can be an important element in the characteristics that employers are looking for and employers preferentially hire domestic workers who are of the same nationality as those they have had previously. Agencies that place domestic workers will then prefer to take people from those countries on to their books. As a result people from other countries find it very difficult even to get interviews for domestic posts and the belief that certain nationalities are good at domestic work becomes self-perpetuating.

Portuguese women are particularly highly regarded as housekeepers in London. They find it easier to get good jobs and can command higher wages or better working conditions than women from other countries. All the formal agencies I interviewed rated Portuguese women as the best housekeepers and one specifically commented on how good all Portuguese women were at ironing, leaving me with an image of Portuguese 'ironing schools' or even an 'ironing czar' making sure all ironing in Portugal was up to a government standard! Filipina women are also considered to be good housekeepers and are popular with employers. The tenacity of these stereo-types about different nationalities was brought home to me when I walked into an upmarket domestic agency in Knightsbridge. I had an appointment to interview one of the partners but the woman on reception did not know I was coming. As I went into the office she visibly stiffened and looked very uncomfortable to see me. I started to think that the agent had changed her mind about talking to me and my interview had been cancelled. When I introduced myself and explained what I was there for, the woman relaxed and smiled. She explained that she had assumed I was looking for a job and a single glance at me, a typically English-looking woman in her mid-twenties, had assured her that she would not have been able to place me. As she explained: 'You can't place English people, they're just not subservient enough.' She went on to say that British people did sometimes come into the agency looking to enter the sector because pay is relatively good and people assume the work is easy. She said she would not even take their details. Restricting people's access to jobs because of their nationality or ethnicity is illegal under equal opportunities legislation but agencies and employers can get around this by asking for characteristics that only people from a certain place are likely to have. As few British women have been working as housekeepers, insisting on many years of experience can exclude British applicants.

Similarly, domestic jobs are highly gendered. Housekeepers, cooks and housekeeper/cooks are, almost without exception, women. This is both because women have traditionally taken on these jobs because it is assumed that they have the right skills and because if men do the tasks involved in these jobs the position is more likely to carry a different title. So a man whose main duties are to cook would be called a 'chef' and a man who ran a household and did cleaning would be a butler or valet. However, the very long tradition of gendered domestic roles that goes back centuries in Britain does mean that men and women tend to have slightly different duties even if their jobs are largely the same.

Butlers

The only jobs that men regularly take on are jobs as gardeners, butlers, valets and chauffeurs. With the exception of gardeners, these jobs are highly prestigious and relatively rare. Gardeners are by no means numerous, but many households employ a gardener part-time or use a gardening service, so this aspect of domestic work is organized like cleaning with most gardeners working for a number of families and very few households having a full-time or live-in gardener.

Butlers are the most prestigious domestic workers, both the highest-paid and the most effective status symbol. A butler can earn as much as a hospital consultant or senior civil servant and will be given comfortable housing, meals and often a car. There are female butlers and butlers from other countries but, unlike housekeepers, British, and more specifically English, people are favoured as butlers to work in Britain and abroad. English butlers are a particularly sought-after status symbol in the United States. Fictional butlers such as the Admirable Crichton and Wodehouse's 'Jeeves' have done much to sustain the image of the perfect butler as an unflappable, discreet and respectful Englishman. Butlers are trained in specialist household management schools or in large formal households where they can rise through the hierarchy. Many are former members of the police or armed forces and they tend to be older than most other domestic workers.

A butler's duties can vary depending on the composition of the family he is working for and the other staff employed. In a large household a butler can have a managerial role, in charge of the overall running of the house and overseeing other staff. A butler would also be expected to be the public face of the household, answering the door or telephone, serving drinks and meals. Butlers can often have responsibility for more personal tasks for male members of the family, such as maintaining clothes or ironing the daily newspaper before it is sent up. In a smaller household a butler would have much more responsibility for day-to-day cleaning and cooking. Some butlers work for a single man and act as combined housekeeper, valet and personal assistant. Many butlers now have role that is close to that of a PA, helping with business affairs as well as domestic ones. One recent ad in *The Lady* magazine described the post as 'butler/housemanager'[8] and an agency described it as 'general factotum'.

Formal work and social life

Domestic workers in formal households often need to be prepared to be highly mobile. Domestic staff can be moved between town and country houses and between main residences and holiday homes all over the world. Employers who regularly spend the weekend in the country and the week in London may employ two separate sets of staff, or at least have some staff permanently based at each house. Or they may require staff to travel between their two houses; driving ahead of them on a Friday evening to the country and on a Sunday evening to town to get ready for their arrival. This type of arrangement can create difficulties for the staff, but is cost efficient for employers. The staff have time taken up with travelling, two houses rather than one to care for, and have their weekends eroded. They may get some time off at each location or may only get one day a week free. Other employers may spend big chunks of the year abroad and expect staff to travel with them. This may sound attractive and perhaps even glamorous and some people do specifically opt for jobs with a lot of travel. However, after a while it can become less desirable as it creates difficulties in establishing and maintaining relationships or even seeing friends regularly.

One way that people can ensure that they maintain some kind of family life despite working in the domestic sector is to work as a 'couple team'. Couples are just what the name implies: a married couple who look after a household between them. Some couples meet in domestic service and then carry on working together. Others decide to enter domestic work after getting married and perhaps raising a family. One couple I interviewed explained that domestic work was a complete change of direction for both of them but they decided to look for jobs as a couple because they were so fed up with never seeing one another. Their children had left home, their house was far too big for just the two of them and they wanted to try something different, so they entered live-in service. They established themselves by first accepting a post with an employer who paid them relatively poorly and worked them hard but in exchange provided them with the training they needed to get a better postion. Couples are paid a single joint wage of around £600–700 per week and are generally assured self-contained housing of a reasonable size.

The 'relaxed rich': domestic employment in informal households

While the size of the ultra-formal domestic sector is quite a surprise in the twenty-first century, it is nothing like as big as the less formal end of the domestic labour market. Informal employers would never dream of asking their domestic workers to wear uniforms but they may nevertheless be able to afford to buy in vast amounts of help to support their lifestyle and enhance their leisure time. More the Islington set than the county set, this group of employers is surprisingly large and surprisingly affluent. They employ nannies, cleaners, au pairs, housekeepers and gardeners but they are not hard-pressed working parents pushed to take on help because of long working hours or a lack of nursery provision. These people are able to employ substantial amounts of domestic help simply because they want to, not because they need to for any reason. Rather than employing the overt status symbol of a formal butler or uniformed housekeeper, these employers are likely to buy in help that maintains status in more subtle ways, for example, by having help with childcare even though one parent is at home, or help with housework to service large houses which are difficult to maintain.

Childcare for the unstressed parent

An advertisement in a recent edition of *The Lady* magazine reads:

> Wanted – Qualified, full time French speaking nanny in SW5 for two very dynamic 1.5 & 2.5 yr old. Full time (11hrs/d + a 1/2d wkds live out) to help mum. Need somebody happy to spend holidays in Europe with us c.12 wks/yr. Must be proactive, imaginative, to be able to distract and occupy them through own initiative. Driving and non-smoker needed with knowledge of London.[9]

Everyone agrees that looking after small children can be hard work, but hiring a full time nanny when a mother is at home is a luxury most families simply cannot afford. The above advertisement stresses that they want a nanny who is 'dynamic', 'imaginative' and 'proactive'; they don't want a nanny who is stuffy and distant or one who is subservient. They are not a formal family – you will help 'mum' yet they are sufficiently well off to afford the salary for a full-time nanny and three months a year abroad. This advertisement is far from rare. Week after week *The Lady*, other publications and myriad web sites carry advertisements for nannies, mothers' helps and au pairs, for families with a mother at home – and it does always seem to be the mother. These families are able to afford the support that many mothers of young children crave. For these families it is possible to give their children all the attention they may need and still have time for leisure.

It is not only large families that take on help despite one parent staying home. Many parents employ help, in the shape of a maternity nurse, from the day they leave hospital with their first child. Maternity nurses work with newborn babies and their mothers, usually for about the first six weeks at home. They are specialist nannies who are on call 24 hours a day to care for the baby and help the new mother. They earn more than other nannies but do not normally work all year because of the demands of the post. Following the maternity nurse, well-off mothers will have a nanny to help them whilst their children are very young and then perhaps switch to a mother's help or au pair when children are a bit older.

Harriet Powell, a mother I interviewed in central London, explained the history of her childcare arrangements. She had two children of secondary school age at the time of the interview and had not worked outside the home since her children were born, except for doing some unpaid charity work. Her husband worked full time and left the childcare and housekeeping arrangements to her. She had arranged a maternity nurse before her first daughter was born but no other childcare after that, imagining she would cope herself. During this early period her mother came to visit and in Harriet's words 'saw what I mess I was in and made me get a nanny'. After the nanny, Harriet employed a series of au pairs and she now has an au pair, who helps out for a day and a half a week, and a cleaner three times a week. Harriet sees these arrangements as perfectly normal. She has less help than her mother would like her to have, less help than some of her friends employ. For Harriet the fact she doesn't work does not mean she has to do everything at home.

Less formal employers may be looking for a different type of nanny than their more formal counterparts. Rather than an English 'Norlander', informal families often take nannies from overseas, particularly from Australia and New Zealand. Young women from these countries can work in Britain under the Working Holidaymaker Scheme and are favoured by many employers because they are imagined to be 'fun-loving'. One agent actually commented that employers used the terms 'formal' and 'informal' to indicate the nationality of nanny that they wanted. 'Formal' meant English or British and 'informal' normally meant new Commonwealth – Australia, New Zealand or Canada (even though the vast majority of British nannies work in less formal situations). Discrimination legislation means that it is illegal to specifically request an employee of a particular nationality or ethnicity or to reject an applicant because of their ethnic background. In domestic employment, presumably like many other sectors, employers put such an emphasis on the nationality of their employees, and associate so many attributes with nationality alone, that agencies find ways of reinterpreting these requests into language that technically obeys the law.

Nannies from overseas are more likely to want to live in than their British counterparts, but they are less likely to be qualified. These are both aspects that can suit families with one parent at home. Parents who are out at work often express anxiety about how their children are being cared for in their absence and whether their nanny is able and experienced enough. Such anxieties can induce them to seek childcarers with extensive experience and professional qualifications. Parents who are at home, however, may feel more comfortable about taking on a nanny without qualifications or with less experience because they will be in the home to supervise and observe their children's care. Well-off families are also more likely to have enough space not to feel invaded by a live-in nanny and to want a nanny who will do housework and evening babysitting, rather than just covering for the hours that parents work.

The relaxed rich also employ mothers' helps and au pairs to do childcare and housework. Mothers' helps are full-time, normally live-in domestic workers who carry out housework and childcare for families with a parent at home. They are not normally trained or qualified and employers are not expected to rely on them for large amounts of care for young children.

More often they do ironing, cleaning, shopping and cooking under the direction of their employer, help care for children while a parent is present and babysit in the evenings. Mothers' helps are paid less than trained nannies and may work longer hours doing heavier work. They are some of the lowest-paid full-time domestic workers (au pairs earn less but are meant to be part-time) and can be expected to do a large amount of work caring for children and looking after a house. Similarly au pairs can be used as housekeepers and babysitters by families who do not rely on them to provide childcare while both parents are working. The au pair's time can be spent doing cleaning and ironing or helping parents feed and bathe children, so allowing a stay-at-home mother to have some leisure time as well as having the house kept to a high standard.

Caring for appearances not children

As well as buying in childcare to create leisure time and a less stressed life, the relaxed rich can buy other forms of help to maintain their houses and make life more comfortable. Cleaners are the most common domestic workers and work for a very wide range of employers for quite different amounts of time each week. Other employers may take on au pairs, housekeepers and even cooks to support an informal but wealthy lifestyle.

Au pairs: Hampstead's dirty little secret?

Au pairs are also employed by wealthy families as an additional form of help alongside other staff. One au pair I interviewed worked as a 'sort of PA' to the woman in a childless couple who also employed a full-time housekeeper. Another worked as a housekeeper for a woman living on her own and another was employed to do housework and dog-walking for a couple without children who also employed a cleaner. A mothers' help or au pair is not the status symbol that a formal domestic worker might be, but employing these forms of help does ensure the maintenance of a way of life that displays prosperity for those who are sensitive to status. A beautifully presented house, that certain ease of living without the constant demands of children or worries about the mountain of ironing waiting at home, and even the leisure time for further consumption, all need other people's labour to sustain them.

Some of the au pairs I interviewed have worked for families who are very wealthy and have lifestyles that are far removed from the majority of the population. One au pair lived in a house with nine bedrooms and seven bathrooms. Another lived in a house so large that she spent five hours every day cleaning one floor of it, while a full-time housekeeper looked after the other floors. Many of the au pairs were in houses that had intercom systems, the modern replacement of the servant's bell, and they would be called by intercom to work in other parts of the house. Only some of the au pairs I interviewed called their employers by their first names and many of them had never spoken to the father in the house.

In theory au pairs are only meant to work for 25 hours per week plus two evenings of babysitting. They are meant to have at least two whole days entirely free each week and have time to pursue their studies. In reality the amount of work au pairs are expected to do varies immensely and what hours they are paid for seems to depend very much on their employer. In a survey of 140 au pairs in London I found that many au pairs reported long working hours but that this did not always result in higher pay. Fewer than 25 per cent of au pairs surveyed reported working only 25 hours a week and 23 per cent worked 40 hours or more (not including babysitting). Six people interviewed reported working more than 50 hours a week and one worked 68 hours. In addition 19 per cent claimed to babysit more than twice a week. Most of the au pairs said they also sometimes did overtime, that is hours over what they regularly did, not hours over their contract, and 52 per cent were not paid any extra for this. The average wage was £50 per week but 8 per cent of those interviewed earned less than £40 per week, 3 per cent earned £100 and the highest wage reported was £200, which was earned by the man who worked 68 hours a week. For au pairs from outside the European Economic Area any overtime was outside the stipulations of their visa. These figures suggest that the label 'au pair' is being given to a range of domestic roles, even those that vary quite dramatically from the part-time, cultural-exchange based idea. This is perhaps because the term 'au pair' is socially acceptable. Employers appear to be taking on an au pair when they want a nanny, housekeeper or both. Rather than admitting to their friends that they have a housekeeper (and running the risk of questions being asked about the housekeeper's visa), employers can call any young foreign woman an au pair and so disguise her real role. Most people are very hazy about the exact nature of the au pair scheme and are happy to accept that young women from foreign countries who do domestic work are 'au pairs'.

Cleaning up

Cleaning and housekeeping are also done by other domestic workers for the relaxed rich. Keeping a pristine house and entertaining lavishly can be important to people in defining their social standing and signalling it to others. Paying for domestic help plays a subtle role in this. Domestic workers can take on the physical stress of housework and they can disguise the amount of effort that has been made, creating an atmosphere of ease and comfort.

Maureen Ind was employed as an informal cook by a media executive living in London. She explained that she had taken the job imagining it to be helping out a stressed working mother who was having trouble coping with the conflicting demands of her family – her own vegetarianism, her husband's low-fat diet and her son's picky eating. After a few weeks in the job, Maureen became aware that her boss entertained frequently and that catering for formal dinner parties and buffets was a regular duty. Maureen realized after overhearing the conversation at one dinner party that she had cooked all the food for, that her employer was taking the credit for the preparation of the meal herself, entirely denying Maureen's existence and all her hard work. Maureen was also expected to do housekeeping that she had not been told about when she took the job. There was a cleaner employed regularly, but Maureen was expected to do other jobs such as cleaning the silver that was on show. Maureen became aware that her job was much more about helping her employer display her taste and status to her friends and much less about helping a busy working mum. She said she realized eventually that her employer was caught in a horrible contradiction:

> She wanted to look like superwoman, like she had done it all herself. But at the same time she would have hated, absolutely hated, the idea that anyone would think she would sit there cleaning her own silver. She wanted people to think she didn't have any help, but then she wouldn't have been able to stand it if they had thought she did her own cleaning.

Maureen's employer wanted her to be invisible, just like Lord Crewe had wanted his housemaids to be invisible to his guests. Employers like these want to present an image to the world that they are not 'dirty'. Their houses are perfectly kept, their precious possessions displayed in pristine condition and all without any effort from anyone. It is as if their status demands not that their houses are cleaned, but that they are inherently clean, free from any kind of pollution or contamination. The hint that these people do have a physical existence that creates dirt is somewhat demeaning to them.

Cleaners

Cleaners are the most numerous domestic workers in Britain. Employed for anything from an afternoon every two weeks, to all day every day, cleaners work for a wide variety of different people. They are employed alongside full-time staff in the most formal households and in addition to other help by wealthy informal employers. They are hired for a few hours a week by working families who are fed up with arguing about the mess or by single people or groups of friends living together who don't want to do the cleaning.

The relaxed rich are perhaps the most important consumers of cleaning labour. In addition to, or sometimes instead of, live-in or full-time help, informal employers consume thousands of hours of help from part-time, live-out cleaners. Cleaners are frontline workers in the battle to present a conspicuously affluent lifestyle to the world. They maintain the products of consumption, the things which are chosen to make life more comfortable or to display taste and affluence to others. Cleaners also make life more comfortable for their employers both in terms of maintaining houses that are pleasant to be in and because employing a cleaner creates leisure time and transfers some of the least satisfying tasks in the house to someone else.

Unlike housekeepers working for the most prestigious formal households, cleaners working for less formal employers would not usually have to worry about vacuuming with the pile of the carpet or preserving precious antique furniture. However, they may be cleaning things that are still very valuable or be trying to maintain very high standards of cleanliness. One employer told me he had had a cleaner who was very good at her job but left because she kept breaking things. As he put it, 'it just happened that everything she broke had cost about a thousand pounds, so it was quite a problem.'

Cleaners working in wealthy informal households may well find that they are faced with houses that are more difficult to keep clean than they would expect. People who know that they can afford to pay someone to do their cleaning can choose to furnish and arrange their houses in a way that is time-consuming to maintain. Being in a position to afford a cleaner actually means that they can choose different furnishing materials or products, such as pale colours or real wood floors[10] and these might be both enjoyable in themselves and indicators of wealth because of the care they demand. Harriet Powell had retained original features of her house, aware that they were time-consuming to clean, and she furnished the house with lots of pictures and Victoriana that also required lots of dusting. She described her house as difficult to clean and saw the solution to this as having a cleaner for more hours a week than she otherwise might have. She did not expect to have to do cleaning herself and therefore didn't think of making the house more manageable.

Jean Rice, another employer I interviewed in central London, who has school age children and does not work outside the home, employs a cleaner to come in twice a week. She explained that the knowledge that she would not have to do all the cleaning and ironing also had an impact on the way the house was used and upon the clothes the whole family wore. Jean hated ironing and so passed this on to her cleaner, who also did some hand washing. As a result Jean choose different clothes when out shopping, she didn't worry if things needed ironing and the whole family had a change of clothes every day. As Jean put it: 'We do tend to have clean clothes every day, a terrible modern thing, you know, everything is always clean. Nobody ever wears trousers twice, or shirts or underwear, so it's like a Chinese laundry.'

The people I interviewed who were happy to arrange their houses and their lives in such a way that they created a lot of work for their cleaners seemed to do so because they assumed they would always be able to employ a cleaner. A number of the women I interviewed explained that they had always employed help because they had never seen housework as their responsibility. This was generally because they had been raised in houses where domestic help was employed and they had been able to pay for help all their adult lives. As Harriet Powell put it when I asked her why she employed someone:

> Why do I employ someone? Well, I employ a cleaner because I hate cleaning and housework. I've never done it because I wasn't brought up that way. You know, I do put things away or whatever. I do clean, but I actually find it boring . . . I can afford it, that's why I employ someone.

Another interviewee explained:

> In terms of cleaning, I haven't cleaned for years, to the extent that when I have to iron something, when I'm going out, I actually quite enjoy ironing a dress . . . But, no, I don't feel that hoovering or washing baths is my job at all.

These women still took responsibility for arranging all the domestic work in their houses and to that extent had not escaped their traditional gender role. They saw themselves, not their husbands, as the person who employed a cleaner and they did all the organizing of finding and paying a cleaner as well as deciding what work she should do. These women used their wealth to transfer the drudgery of housework on to other women but did not challenge the gendered nature of domestic responsibilities nor question whether housework was really that important at all.

Men, cleaning and cleaners

It is not only some well-off women who do not see cleaning as their responsibility. Men are a growing group in the employment of cleaners and single men seem to be more likely to employ a cleaner than are single women. Demographic trends have created many more households of single people and groups of independent individuals living together. Some single women do employ cleaners, but men seem to be more likely to, perhaps because they earn more on average and are less conditioned to think they should do housework. Men do not see why they should do cleaning and they don't always know how to do it. Households of single people living together can be prime candidates for buying in help as they have high incomes and the potential for disagreements about mess in shared spaces is huge. I interviewed Neil Wells, who had employed a cleaner when living with three male friends. I asked about why they had decided to do this. He explained that they were all working long hours and none of them took any interest in keeping the house clean. As Neil put it, as they were four men, 'there were not a lot of cleaning genes between them.' The suggestion was made that they should get a cleaner and split the cost four ways. Neil explained the decision was easily taken:

> I work my socks off, sort of 50 to 60 hours a week at the moment. The last thing I want to do when I come home is mess around with a hoover or something for the sake of a fiver. It's just an absolute bargain.

Neil and his friends seemed to have no real idea how to clean or how to stop a house becoming a disaster zone. He talked with wonder about all the different cleaning products that their cleaner used and expressed surprise when these ran out and she needed money to buy more. He also marvelled at the effects of her visits, seeming able to describe the work she had to do but then being quite vague about what cleaning actually involved and apparently not able to see how he and his friends could have done this themselves:

> What she did was fantastic though. We left the place in a complete tip. By Wednesday of each week it was a disaster and she'd come in and clean up all the kitchen, the living room, the bathrooms and so on. I think she probably knocked through it in two and a half hours and be out of the house. No one was ever supervising her . . . She did all the communal rooms, the living room, the kitchen with a sort of a dining room bit on the end, the hallway, the stairs, there was a bathroom and

a separate toilet room as well . . . In the kitchen there hadn't been any washing up done for four or five days so there was just piles all along [the counter] and obviously, no cleaning was ever done to anything like the cooker or the fridge or the grill or anything like that. Basically she'd do all the washing up that was left. There was also lots of take away, bags kicking around so obviously she'd get rid of those, clean all the surfaces, give the place a scrub. Then in the living room there'd be loads of papers lying around, she'd tidy it up, give it a hoover, get rid of any old mugs lying around. Then obviously the bathroom would always be in a bit of a state so she'd do all that, get the Dettol out, or whatever it is. She always left the place really nice . . . Also, if you timed it right and did your washing for the day before she came in and you were organized, she'd iron your shirts as well.

Neil didn't seem to be a particularly useless young man; he was probably more typical than exceptional. He had gone from living at home, looked after by mum, to a student house and then to sharing with friends. Along the way he had gathered a bit of knowledge about hoovering and washing up and was good at looking after his smart clothes for work, but other forms of cleaning were rather mysterious to him. By the time of the interview Neil was living with his girlfriend, who seemed keen to demystify this world for him, so perhaps he will learn what Dettol is for.

Being too important to deal with dirt

As Neil's description of why he and his friends got a cleaner suggests, another reason why many people employ cleaners is to create more time for leisure. As average working hours have increased, so has the gap between the incomes of the highest and lowest paid. This means that for many working people the cost of some other people's labour is relatively cheap – 'an absolute bargain' in Neil's words. What these people don't have is much spare time but they do have the money to buy in other people to do some of the things they don't want to do. When I interviewed people who employed cleaners, the value of their time was the reason most likely to be given for employing someone to do housework. As one person put it: 'I'm desperate about my time.' This was most clearly the case for people who were working long hours but it was also the logic used by people who appeared to have more time available. So, people who themselves worked part time, or did not work outside the home, still said that their time was too valuable to be spent doing cleaning. This reflects the widely held but contradictory idea that cleaning needs to be done but is also somehow unimportant. It also echoes the notion that modern life is especially busy and fraught for everyone. In reality different people face very different demands on their time and the 'work rich', as they are so often called, are only one sub-group of the rich or of the hardworking. One of the things that is overlooked is people's expectations for leisure. These are expectations that better-off people may be able to meet by employing domestic help. They are likely to look more like distant dreams to the people they are employing.

Related to many people's desire to pass on domestic tasks because they think there is something better they could be doing is the fact that many people don't like doing housework. One outcome of this is that people pass on to cleaners not the tasks that are most important, or even those they consider the hardest physically, or the most skilled. They pass on the things they least like doing themselves. For most people this seems to be ironing but everyone I interviewed had their own bugbears that they got their cleaner to do, from vacuuming the stairs (four flights in total) to cleaning the bath or polishing the brass on the front door.

The fact that people don't like doing housework might seem like an obvious point, but it is worth a bit of examination. People explain their dislike of housework by pointing out that it is hard work, that it is repetitive and can be deeply unsatisfying because as soon as you have done it the other members of your household have managed to undo it again. All of this is true, but is housework intrinsically any more difficult or unsatisfying than shopping (one of our favourite leisure activities) or gardening (the 'new sex')? Or is it the case that people's attitudes towards doing housework reflect the very low value put on it socially? It is not valued by society and neither is it valued by the people who do it or the people for whom it is done. But for some reason we still consider housework to be largely necessary and its completion desirable. The value placed on domestic work also transfers to the people who do that work, whether they are paid or unpaid. The women's movement campaigned for years to have the work women do within their homes recognized as valuable and as real work. For some feminists this meant it deserved real pay.[11] Domestic workers also suffer from the assumption that their work is somehow less 'real' than other forms of labour. Whilst employers think of housework as too time-consuming to do themselves they seem to suddenly find the same work insubstantial when others do it.

Status and cruelty: the treatment of paid domestic workers

One outcome of the low status of domestic work is that domestic workers may be treated very badly by employers, and sometimes as less than human. Live-in domestic workers are particularly susceptible to abuse since employers can control their entire lives – where they live, whom they know, how much they sleep and even what they eat. Those domestic workers who are particularly dependent on their employers, because of their immigration status, their desperate need to earn money or obligations through family ties, can be even more vulnerable. A large number of studies have shown that in situations where employers are able to mistreat domestic workers, because they are unlikely to be detected or punished if discovered, then many of them do. This is a shocking idea and not one that many people want to think about. Bridget Anderson, who has studied the lives of domestic workers throughout Europe and worked with domestic workers who have escaped abusive employers in Britain, has highlighted the importance of domestic workers as 'status-givers' to their employers. Somehow employers enhance their own status by using the labour of their domestic workers and by demeaning them as people, even to the point of imprisoning them and beating them.

The humiliating treatment of domestic workers seems to be designed to mark their difference from the family they work for despite their inclusion within family space. One worker quoted by Anderson recounted the way that she was treated as if she were diseased and as if she had no physical needs:

> As soon as I came to London and to her house I feel like she brought me to jail . . . I have to sleep on a shelf, which is made to keep all the things, suitcases, everything . . . So morning 4.30 to midnight I have to be up. I have no rest and no place to sit. She ask me not to sit on the chair, not to be near the children. Everytime I go to the toilet I have to wash with Dettol and all and not touch anything about the children. She treat me as if I have bad disease.[12]

The domestic worker is treated as if she were physically different from the employing family, as if somehow she is not the same kind of thinking and feeling being as they are. Domestic workers can be denied sufficient sleep and food, may be physically and psychologically abused, denied time off and kept from leaving the house or speaking to other people freely.[13] Some of these restrictions resemble those that Victorian and earlier employers subjected their servants to, monitoring every aspect of their lives and denying that they had 'finer feelings'. They are also similar to slave owners' attitudes towards their slaves. Slave ownership was long justified on the basis that slaves were racially inferior, not equally human as their masters, and unable to look after themselves if independent.

As the information collected by the campaigning group Kalayaan shows, abuse of domestic workers is widespread when those workers are in a situation that makes escape or complaint difficult or near impossible. Studies of domestic workers in other countries have shown that abuse is not reserved for one group of workers or carried out by one group of employers. Joy Zarembka has revealed that United States immigration policy allows foreign nationals, diplomats, officials of international agencies such as the World Bank and some US citizens with permanent residency abroad to import domestic workers on visas that prohibit them from changing employers. Each year over 200,000 domestic workers enter the US on such visas and no records are kept of their whereabouts. These visa arrangements mean domestic workers are unable to report abuse or leave abusive employers. If they do leave the employer they are registered to, they are considered 'out of status' and liable for immediate deportation. Joy Zarembka found instances of abuse of domestic workers by some of the wealthiest residents of Washington DC. She records a Bolivian woman forced to work over 12 hours a day and imprisoned by a human rights lawyer, who also refused to allow her hospital treatment after she was raped. A World Bank official forced his domestic worker to work 24 hours a day with no time off, beat her and imprisoned her when she tried to report the beatings. Others endured humiliations such as being addressed as 'the creature' or 'the slave', being made to kiss an employer's feet and one domestic worker was made to wear a dog collar at all times and sleep outdoors with her employer's dogs.[14]

These examples show that the legal standing of domestic workers, particularly those with precarious immigration status, can create a context within which employers feel able to abuse their employees without risk of punishment. It is also true, however, that employers of more secure domestic workers may treat their employees badly, even if they do not physically abuse them or imprison them, and this may also be a way of demonstrating their status and power.

In *The Nanny Diaries*[15] a fictionalized account of real experiences of nannying, Nicola Kraus and Emma McLaughlin demonstrate superbly the tense relationships within which domestic employment takes place. In the diaries 'Nanny' works for Mr and Mrs X, a wealthy New York couple with a young son. Mrs X does not work but spends her days lunching, going to the beautician and planning ways in which she can cement or improve her social status. Her status, however, depends entirely on her husband and she knows her position is precarious. She married him after they had an affair while he was married to his first wife and she now suspects she might herself be being replaced. The help that Mrs X employs – Nanny, a housekeeper and various personal advisors – are her army in her struggle for status. They give her the leisure that allows her to mix in the 'right' circles; they help her to display her wealth and to host events designed to impress.

But Mrs X also uses her employees in order to feel better about herself. She treats them capriciously, changing their hours, denigrating their achievements, overlooking their work and ultimately sacking Nanny on a whim. The domestic workers are the only people she has any real power over in her life. She wants to think of herself as a high-status, important woman but it is only in her relationship with her employees that this is realized and so she demonstrates this power whenever she can.

Although it is a novel, *The Nanny Diaries* illuminates the way that domestic workers are entangled in their employers' social status. It is particularly effective at exposing the contradictory and precarious status of wealthy women who do not have an income of their own. Their access to a high income appears to give them power and independence but their reliance on their husband's wealth undermines this, making them more vulnerable than other women they normally look down upon. Traditional gender roles create this situation and also mean its effects are acted out on a domestic stage when female employers use their power within the household to demean their employees and so fortify themselves.

Pamela Sambrook, in her examination of country house servants in the seventeenth to nineteenth centuries, remarked that the purpose of cleaning was to indicate status. Cleanliness marked higher social status in a world where achieving it was difficult. The purpose of servants was to deliver that cleanliness, so demonstrating their employers' standing to the world.[16] Some servants, most notably footmen, displayed their employer's status through their physical presence and appearance, and they were clothed to show this to the greatest extent. Other household servants were employed to create an environment that was comfortable and that would clearly signal the high standing of the householders, through ensuring near-unattainable cleanliness and by caring for all their employer's goods, both of which were such important markers of rank.

This aspect of domestic labour is rarely mentioned today. Domestic employment is presumed to have grown because of demand from over-stretched working mothers, or work-rich time-poor executives. The truth is that much paid domestic labour is still about reproducing status differentials. Domestic workers today care for their employers' consumer goods just like they did in the past. They clean their houses and press their clothes so they look impressive to the rest of the world. Domestic workers free their employers to spend more time on leisure, decorate their homes however they please, to entertain lavishly and to wear clothes that are time-consuming to care for; even to pretend they are a 'superwoman'. All these things are possible because of the labour of domestic workers. For some domestic employers these labours are not enough and they feel the need to enhance their own status by denigrating their workers, humiliating them and abusing them. Their ability to do this to another human being shows their power, their wealth and, of course, their inhumanity. It also shows us how little things have really changed.

6 | A life between slavery and luxury
Living as a domestic worker

Historians commenting on the lives of servants in affluent households in the past have noted that one of the unique aspects of servant experience was that they lived in the midst of astounding wealth but had nothing – sometimes not even a bed to sleep on – themselves. Servants' familiarity with the lifestyles of their employers and their awareness of their employers' wealth and their own poverty are cited as bases for resentment and defiance. For many domestic workers today the contradictions are greater. An au pair, for example, may live in a comfortable room with en suite bathroom in a house that cost several million pounds. She may eat with her employers, sit and watch television with them or even go on holiday with them. But she is still their employee and has nothing herself. Earning just £50 per week she cannot afford to eat out with friends or buy new clothes and when she returns home it will probably be by long-distance coach because she cannot afford the airfare.

This chapter examines the experiences of domestic workers living and working in Britain. It gives details about working hours, typical pay, the type of work done and the emotional complexities of working and living in someone else's home. It concentrates on the experiences of cleaners, nannies and au pairs, i.e. some of the most numerous domestic workers, and uses interview material to illustrate general trends with individual experiences.

Au pairs are one of the fastest growing groups of domestic workers and the lowest paid, earning less than £2 an hour on average. Nannies can be qualified and quite well paid but may work long hours and suffer from isolation, particularly when they are far from home. Cleaners are often benefit-dependent women drawn into the informal sector because of the poverty trap. They do work that is low status and stigmatized but not always poorly paid. Nannies and au pairs tend to live in employers' homes and have responsibility for childcare. Live-in jobs can bring their own complications: live-in domestic workers are unable to 'go home' at the end of a working day, and employers feel 'invaded' by their employee. In the most extreme cases employees can easily steal from their employers or damage their property, whilst employers can abuse or assault domestic workers with little fear of detection. More often, the stresses and strains of sharing space means that it is hard for workers to limit their working hours and employers feel that their homes are not their own.

Pay and working conditions

As shown earlier, domestic labour is typically poorly paid and has low status. Some domestic workers may earn nothing at all except their keep and many earn less than the legal minimum wage.[1] Basic pay, however, may not be the problem with remuneration for domestic workers – other elements may be more important in bringing down domestic workers' incomes relative to other jobs and in differentiating between domestic positions. Payments in kind, the standard of accommodation provided, the amount of work demanded, entitlements to holiday pay and sick pay all vary substantially between employers and can have a profound impact on what domestic workers really earn.

Au pairs

Au pairs' pay is relatively standardized but there are still large differences in what au pairs receive from different employers. As they live in, the accommodation provided is an extremely important element of their remuneration and this can vary from a shared room to a self-contained flat. The amount of work au pairs are expected to do also varies and whether they are paid for extra work is important. Employers will also sometimes cover costs that au pairs incur and this can be worth more than their standard pay.

Au pairs are not officially employees but rather are considered as family members. Their pay is called 'pocket money' and the level is recommend by the Home Office as £45 per week. Au pairs do not have any other entitlements, their employers do not pay tax or National Insurance for them and as a result au pairs cannot claim any benefits if sick or unemployed and those from outside the EU can only receive medical treatment from the National Health Service in an emergency. The average au pair in London is paid about £50 per week and may also be given something towards travel costs. Outside London pay is slightly lower and there is less pressure on employers to subsidize travel.

Au pairs are meant to be actively involved in learning English and the most obvious way to do this is to enrol in English language classes at specialist schools. School fees are about £100–200 per month and so represent a substantial outgoing to the average au pair. Some employers pay for their au pair's classes and this can be one of the most important differences between jobs. Other costs that some employers will meet include things like regular telephone calls home, the cost of travel home once a year, day trips to other places in Britain and provision of a mobile phone. In rare cases employers have paid for driving lessons for their au pairs and the costs of running a car for the au pair to use. Some employers will take au pairs on holiday with them and pay for this, but this is normally because the au pair is needed for childcare during the holidays rather than as an act of selfless generosity.

Organizing and keeping control of free time can be quite a problem for some au pairs. Living in their employer's home means they are always available when extra work crops up. Lots of au pairs reported that they were asked to do extra work or babysitting at short notice, or to do tasks outside their remit by employers. One au pair, Lisa, described how the 'family' relationship that au pairs are meant to have with their employers puts pressure on au pairs to work outside their hours and that little things continually eat into what is meant to be free time:

> The mother is so busy she doesn't manage to do the shopping properly somehow, which means that I often have to pick things up and she asks me to go out and buy things. When she is going shopping it has to be quick, quick, quick so I have to go with her to help her which is annoying sometimes when it's in the morning in my free time. Once she asked me on the weekend if I could go shopping with her and I can't say no.

Few au pairs found it easy, or even possible, to counter the demands made by their employers. Instead they preferred to keep their heads down and focus on their futures and the skills they were trying to acquire in Britain. At worst, demands from employers can be nearly constant and au pairs can be severely overworked and exploited. Katerina Bose, an au pair from the Czech Republic, described the emotional blackmail used by her employer to prevent her taking time off:

> I am so ashamed because I always thought I would be able to fight for truth and for justice and I won't ever keep my mouth shut. And now in my own job I am afraid to ask for one day off because I know at once she will be in a bad mood at once. So I'd rather keep my mouth shut,

not to have problems there and I'm so ashamed, I hate myself for that . . . I asked for holidays because I was very tired, from February I didn't have a single whole day off so I decided to take four days off and I asked for them . . . She wasn't very satisfied but she won't be because she isn't direct, she doesn't say 'I don't want it'. Actually she allows me everything I ask for but it's up to me to have the courage to ask because she allows it but then she behaves so horribly . . . In this job you have to show how far they [the employer] can go because if you don't show this, and all the girls agree on this, they will take advantage of you as much as they can . . . Really, we would have worked for them from the very [early] morning till late at night and they wouldn't even care.

Katerina blamed herself for the situation she was in because she had not had the courage to face her employer's sulking. But trying to live in a house where there is a bad atmosphere is very hard and her employer was probably well aware that most au pairs would rather avoid such a situation. Her comment that 'all the girls agree' shows that her experience of pushy employers was not isolated. Katerina buoyed herself up by thinking about her improved prospects when she returned to the Czech Republic. She wanted to teach English in her local school and said that whenever she felt sad she said to herself, 'I have to do it for my children at school . . . that's my motivation.' The need to learn English in order to improve job prospects at home, and the large amount of money that au pairs invested in English classes, meant that they were under quite a lot of pressure to remain in Britain. Rather than being carefree students who were just working abroad for fun, the au pairs interviewed needed their jobs and would put up with quite a lot to keep them.

As well as the number of working hours each week being quite uneven for au pairs as a group, the number of weeks that au pairs were expected to work each year also varied with employers. In general, au pairs did not get any holiday unless their employers went away, i.e. they had no rights to any leave at a time of their choice. Those au pairs whose employers did not go away on holiday, or who took their au pairs with them but expected them to work, did not get any holiday. Those au pairs who remained behind when their employers went on holiday got some kind of a break. Some used this time to go home, some to travel around Britain. Others stayed in their employer's home and still had some work to do. In general, the issue of holiday entitlement did not seem to be much of a problem because many au pairs only stay in post for part of the year and may get a break before or after au pairing. However, for those au pairs who work solidly for a whole year, or maybe longer, it could be quite a problem.

Living in can make it difficult if an au pair is ill. Unlike in a regular job when someone would phone in sick and then have the right to sick pay or to claim sickness benefit, au pairs cannot get away from their workplace. Katerina explained what had happened to her and said that it was typical of the experiences of the au pairs that she knew:

> Once I was ill, I had Saturday off. I came down and it was the first, for the first time I wanted to stay home because I was not feeling well. I wanted to sleep or something. I came downstairs into the kitchen to have tea or coffee and she began to, the lady began to ask me to do some work there. They really don't realize . . . I couldn't believe it. She knows I am ill. I am feeling horrible, but as soon as I appear in the kitchen I am dragged into the work.

So Katerina was expected to work despite the fact that she was ill and it was her day off. As she saw it her employers just didn't think about the fact that for her it was work. Other employers might be more sensitive, but an au pair who was ill or incapacitated for any length of time would be expected to go home, rather than being looked after by her employers. As some au pairs have to pay to access medical treatment in the UK they might also prefer to go home.

Many au pairs take on second jobs to increase their earnings. The au pairs interviewed did cleaning and babysitting for neighbours or worked in restaurants or bars in the evenings. For those from outside the EEA, this work was outside the terms of their visa, as was any overtime they did for their employing family. Agents interviewed commented that it was common for au pairs to ask for longer working hours so they could earn more money, and would ask for a job that is often called an 'au pair plus', something that is completely beyond the terms of the au pair arrangement. Agents also said that almost all au pairs took on extra work and this was sometimes organized by their main employers who would 'loan them out' to friends to babysit or clean, sometimes taking a cut of their earnings in exchange for making such arrangements.

Accommodation is a very important aspect of how au pairs are treated. The Home Office stipulates that au pairs should be given at least their own room, rather than sharing with the children they are caring for, and almost all au pairs are given this. The need for extra space restricts who can take on an au pair more than the cost of wages, particularly in places like London where housing is very expensive and families struggle to afford accommodation that is big enough just for them without thinking about housing an au pair too. However, some au pair employers are very wealthy, or they have large houses because they have inherited them or were able to buy them when prices were lower. This means that some au pairs are given much more than the bare minimum and many have their own bathrooms as well as bedrooms, even their own flats.

Au pairs may not necessarily want jobs that have the largest accommodation. Some prefer to be more involved with the family and more included in their space. Employers may make an au pair's room particularly comfortable or give them more space so that they do not need to use other rooms in the house. One employer explained this, saying:

> I always gave them a big room and I gave them a telly and I'd say to them, 'If ever we're in the sitting room *don't* feel free to come in.' Whereas lots of people say, you know, the au pair deal is that they're supposed to be part of the family, and I'd say, 'You're not. If you want a buddy-buddy family then we're not the family for you.'

A whole flat may not be the benefit it first seems if employers put restrictions on how au pairs use that space. Only a minority of au pairs seem to be free to invite friends home whenever they want to and one au pair who was interviewed and had her own flat in a wing of the house reported that her employers still asked her to come in and out through the main front door of the house so they knew where she was.

The working conditions au pairs experience in Britain are a result partly of their own dependence on employers because of their need to learn English and partly of employers' working conditions, such as long or irregular hours, which can be transferred into the home. The au pairs surveyed were very highly motivated to learn English and this had an impact on the hours they would work and the treatment they tolerated. All those interviewed paid their own school fees and saved what money they could so that they could attend classes for as many hours as possible. Employers who rely on au pairs for childcare because they go out to work can force their au pairs to be very flexible and can make demands on their time at short notice. If their own work demands flexibility, late meetings, last-minute changes to deadlines or whatever, they can pass these demands back to their au pairs by requiring them to work for longer in the evenings or at weekends. However, employers who work long hours are not necessarily the most demanding. Katerina Bose, who had not had a single day off in more than four months, worked for a family where the mother worked part time and which also employed a full-time housekeeper.

Nannies

In contrast to au pairs, nannies are likely to be officially employed, paid a regular salary and have their tax and National Insurance paid. Some nannies do work 'off the books', and instances have been found of employers lying to nannies about keeping up their tax and National Insurance payments[2] but it seems that the majority of nannies are formally employed. One boost to this has been a recent change in regulations for Working Tax Credit which can now be paid towards the cost of a nanny if that nanny is registered and inspected by the Office for Standards in Education (Ofsted). Although very few employers are going to be using benefits to pay for a nanny, even to apply for them an employee's status would have to be absolutely above board. Nannies are also likely to be found through agencies and a reputable agency will make it clear to an employer what their responsibilities are as well as letting a nanny know their rights.

Nannies' pay varies depending on whether they live in or live out, on whether they are qualified or not, and by region. In areas where there is a general shortage of qualified nannies pay rates will go up. Some employers will also pay nannies more for looking after more children, but strangely, employers who expect a nanny to do other duties, such as housekeeping, often pay the least. By law, nannies must be paid at least the national minimum wage appropriate for their age group: £4.10 per hour for 18- to 21-year olds and £4.85 per hour for people over 21, that is £194 for a 40-hour week. However, some employers make deductions for payments in kind when nannies live in, calculating an amount for rent, food or bills. Yet according to official guidelines payments in kind are not supposed to be counted against the minimum wage. The government provides specific guidance that food cannot be considered as payment for the purposes of minimum wage calculations and even provision of accommodation should only be considered as worth £3.75 per day or £26.25 per week.[3] Of course there are employers who do not know these rules and others who do not care to find them out. Most nannies, however, earn more than the minimum wage and those who are qualified and live out are likely to earn twice as much.

Nannies who are qualified, experienced and can provide good references (particularly from local families) are treated as professionals who do not do general cleaning but are expected to design programmes of stimulating activities for their charges. These nannies can earn more than they would working for a private or local authority nursery and may get other benefits such as their own car. The most ambitious parents can, however, be rather demanding in terms of the activities they expect their nannies to include in a regular schedule. Nicola Kraus and Emma McLaughlin's fictional nanny is expected to take her 4 year-old charge to music classes, swimming lessons, physical education and karate, joining in with every class. She is also meant to talk to him in French one day a week and is criticized for not being able to teach him Latin.[4] Real parents might not make quite such incredible demands but some parents do prepare their children for the increasingly competitive school system early and expect nannies to do their part to coach children for entrance exams.

The important aspects of a nanny's pay and conditions that vary between employers are things such as hours worked and how flexible these are, holiday entitlements and recognition of the expenses a nanny may incur while doing her job. Nannies tend to work long hours because their working day has to include their employer's travel time as well as the hours they are at work (if their employer does go out to work). Even employers who do not work quite often want a nanny who will help give the children breakfast and perhaps take one of them to school or nursery first thing in the morning and also still be there to help with teatime in the evening. Nannies who live-in are also called on to babysit and some employers expect a live-in nanny to get up in the night if one of the children wants something. These expectations mean that long hours can be one of the most difficult parts of the job. Nannies are also expected to be flexible, particularly if their employers are out at work and themselves face last minute demands. The difference between an employer who does not suddenly expect their nanny to drop everything and look after the children for another two hours because they are busy and one who does can be more important in making a job bearable than the rate of pay or even the basic hours.

Negotiating holiday pay and entitlement can be a sticky area in nanny employment. The European Working Time Directive dictates that all employees have the right to at least four weeks' holiday each year. Most employers give this, often because they take at least that much holiday themselves, but expecting a nanny to arrange holidays around the family does have its problems. In the first place, nannies who are taken on holiday by their employers to continue their childcare duties can face the same problem as au pairs who are taken on holiday: their employers assume that their nanny has had a holiday because they have. They think they have been terribly generous paying for her to go to their nice resort and entirely overlook the fact that she has actually been working flat out so that *they* can have a break. Even for nannies who do get time off when their employers go away, there is a question about how fair it is for nannies to have no choice over when they get time off. Bea Smith, a nanny working in central London caring for two pre-school age children, explained her situation to me. She had been working for the same family, the Kearns, since the first child was born and got on with her employers very well. They were a relatively young and clearly successful couple and Bea admired what they had achieved. She was relatively well paid and, she explained, she got quite a few weeks off every year when the family went away. However, as time had gone on Bea had noticed that this wasn't actually always a benefit because she could never choose when she had a break. As she put it:

They take quite a lot of holidays in the year. For example, January, end of January, they went to Tenerife, then they went off to America the other day and in between they went to Disney, so they travel a lot. You see, I do get a lot of holidays. But, at the end of the day, when you look at it, it's not my holiday, it's their holiday. So while they're both working, they can afford to say, 'Yeah we're going here and there.' I might not have the money to go [at that time].

Bea had managed to negotiate with her employers by explaining this to them and had agreed on some holiday that was 'hers' to take when she wanted or needed to. It might seem like a small point if a nanny is being given six or seven weeks off each year, but being in a job where you do not have any leave that you can take when you want to is quite a disadvantage.

Bea also explained that the Kearns' generosity with basic pay had made it awkward for her to talk to them about other costs she thought they should cover. The Kearns thought they were being generous, paying above average, but Bea thought there was a principle involved similar to that surrounding her right to holiday. This came out in a discussion of her car and the expenses related to it. Bea thought her car was necessary for work. She used it to take one of the children to and from nursery every day and used it to run errands or take the children to activities. Bea had owned a car before she started the job and was very attached to her current car, things which the Kearns took as evidence that her car was nothing to do with them. After two years of disagreement about the car Bea won out and her employers started to pay her money for petrol and something towards her tax and car insurance. Bea felt victorious but it was clear that the dispute had had an impact on the relationship between Bea and the Kearns. A conversation with Moira Kearns also made it to clear to me that they considered the petrol and insurance payments to be a pay rise for Bea, rather than her due on principle.

These kinds of details are normally sorted in an employment situation. Even quite small employers would have some kind of policy on expenses or essential car use and very few companies would take someone on and then tell them they'll let them know when they can have a holiday but they don't know how many weeks a year it will be and they won't always get much notice. These issues get overlooked in nanny employment both because the home is not a typical workplace and the demands put on nannies may not be easy to predict: and because employers can forget that while caring for their children might be a pleasure for them (or at least just part of family life), for their nanny it is a *job* and should be organized as such.

Cleaners

It is clear from previous chapters that cleaners are an overlooked group of domestic workers, a group who particularly suffer from their work not being considered as 'real work' and from being invisible to their employers unless there's a problem. They are also perhaps the most numerous domestic workers but estimates of their numbers are also the most difficult.

On the other hand, cleaners have more autonomy than other domestic workers, are not so easily embroiled in the emotional trials and tribulations that live-in workers face, can live with their own families and, on the face of it, are relatively well paid. As a junior university lecturer in the mid 1990s I was earning substantially less per hour than the cleaners I interviewed in central London. After my Dean cheerfully remarked to me, at the time I was doing this fieldwork, that he saw 'no reason why [I] should not work 70 hours a week', becoming a cleaner looked increasingly attractive!

Cleaning is taken on by people, mostly women, who particularly want informal sector work. As outlined in Chapter 3, people who receive state benefits but still have caring responsibilities at home can gain the most from working in a sector which is off the records and quite flexible in terms of hours. Other groups that take on cleaning work include students, often foreign students who have restrictions on the hours they are allowed to work, people whose immigration status restricts them working in the formal sector, and people who do not want to go through formal application procedures perhaps because their written English isn't very good.

Being able to work 'off the books' appears to be an opportunity for people who would otherwise be in the poverty trap. A number of cleaners thought their pay was higher than it would be in a 'proper' job, and certainly some employers considered that having a cleaner was a good thing to do because of the help it gave to impoverished women without any other chance of employment. However, there are real limitations associated with working in the informal sector, much apart from running the risk of detection and castigation. One aspect of this is that cleaners who do not pay National Insurance contributions will not be able to access some benefits. This may not be a problem for many years but would, for example, reduce their pension entitlement in the future. Not having any official record of earnings can also make it difficult to establish a credit record. Cleaners who need to borrow money may be forced to pay higher rates of interest because of this and would probably find it impossible to get credit for large purchases. In addition to these specific problems the informal nature of cleaning infuses its entire organization and leaves cleaners without rights. The way cleaners are hired, fired and treated in between reflects employers' belief that they are 'self-employed' and that employers have no responsibility to worry about their working conditions.

Pay rates in cleaning are kept up in middle-class areas where there is lots of work but fewer people who are looking for cleaning work. In these areas cleaning can be particularly lucrative for women who establish a reputation with a group of local employers. Employers want cleaners who are reliable and whom they can trust in their houses and this shapes who can access work as a cleaner. Employers' worries about whom they can trust mean that new cleaners may find it difficult to find work in an area and those cleaners who already have work, and therefore references, find it easiest to get more. This can mean it is difficult for people to break into cleaning but that once they have the experience, contacts and references in a local area, they will have an over-supply of work.

Cleaners often find work, and employers often find cleaners, through personal contacts and word of mouth. This leads to informal networks of cleaners and employers developing that can then dominate the labour market in an area. Cleaners who are not in on the networks find it difficult to get work, and employers who are outside the loop find it hard to get a cleaner. Cleaners will quite often pass the names of employers to their friends or relatives if they have too much work and in some areas this leads to groups of cleaners of one nationality dominating. So one small area might have large numbers of Colombian cleaners while the next area has Polish or Filipina cleaners. Cleaners will also discuss their pay and perks and ask one employer for benefits that they get with another. Employers will ask friends and neighbours for advice about appropriate pay and conditions for cleaners. Again this can have the effect of creating distinct local areas with their own practices which differ slightly in their norms from the areas near by.

Basic pay rates are kept up by the shortage of cleaners in well-off areas and can be lower in areas with less demand. Cleaners tend to be paid at least legal minimum wage and when this was introduced it was a useful bargaining tool for cleaners who were poorly paid even though they work off the books and would not be in a position to go to a tribunal to enforce their rights. Employers tend to take the line that their cleaners are 'self-employed', in the belief that this makes paying tax or National Insurance the cleaner's not the employer's responsibility. Given this rhetoric, an employer would not be able to deny a cleaner the minimum wage and still portray him- or herself as keeping within the law. In practice most cleaners earn more than this and in areas of high demand in central London and other big cities they could easily earn twice as much.

While basic pay is relatively high compared to other 'unskilled' work, cleaners can lose out compared to formally employed staff in other ways.

Employers' tendency to overlook the fact that cleaning is a job can result in infrequent pay rises, no sick pay or holiday pay, and with cleaners having their hours cut or work increased without compensation. I found great inconsistencies in employers' attitudes towards pay rises, holidays and holiday pay and sick pay for their cleaners. Harriet Powell, who employed a cleaner to come in three times a week, paid her cleaner if she was off ill, if she took holiday, if the Powells were away on holiday and she paid her double at Christmas. She also gave her cleaner regular pay rises when the cleaner asked. By contrast, Bea Smith's employer, Moira Kearns, who also employed a cleaner for nine hours a week, only paid a bit of holiday pay and said she would pay sick pay if her cleaner was off for a long time and asked for it. Other employers said they would pay none at all and some cleaners lost out because they sent a friend as a replacement if they were away or ill and that person got paid instead. None of the people I interviewed who employed a cleaner had thought of giving their cleaner a pay rise annually on a specific date. It seems that few employers approach taking on a cleaner in a systematic way and think through the basic things like when to give a pay rise, or how to organize holidays. Employers that I interviewed were surprised when I mentioned 'sick pay', as if it were irrelevant to them despite their role as employers.

Despite not being quite comfortable with their role as employers, many people who hire cleaners make efforts to monitor their cleaner's work and try to make sure they are getting what they see as their money's worth. Few employers are in the house while their cleaner is working. Those who go out to work always arrange for the cleaner to come while they are at work. People who don't go out to work generally find something to do outside the house while the cleaner is there. This means that employers normally have to trust their cleaners to hold a set of their house keys and to have access to all their things in their absence. It also means that employers cannot see their cleaners working and this causes many of them to think that their cleaners do not spend as long cleaning as they are paid for. It was a common refrain amongst the employers I interviewed that 'She doesn't take that long.' It seems ironic that people who employed someone to do a job they considered far too arduous or time-consuming to do themselves also simultaneously thought that their cleaner whipped through the work in no time at all, yet still they did not consider their cleaner to be highly skilled or particularly able! Some employers coped with their anxiety about their cleaners' working hours by trying to monitor them, 'popping' back home because they had 'forgotten' something or asking a neighbour to notice when the cleaner left. Others asked their cleaner to do more work and would leave extra ironing or notes asking for specific things to be done. Neil Wells, who, with the three friends he lived with, employed a cleaner to keep all the communal spaces in the house clean, thought that his cleaner probably left an hour or an hour and a half early every week. But he didn't mind because she did what she was paid for. Few other employers seemed happy to take this attitude, so their cleaners risked having the demands put on them increased or even the hours they were paid for cut.

Leaving

Almost all domestic workers suffer from insecurity of employment. Groups such as cleaners or au pairs work outside the normal bounds of employment and have few rights under the law, although they have much more protection than most of them realize.[5] Even formally employed nannies or housekeepers find it difficult to enforce their rights. They are usually isolated within a house and would have little evidence to show for the way they have been treated. Normal practice within the domestic sector is that employers sack domestic workers with little notice and for no particular reason and that domestic workers leave employers with just as little ceremony.

An 'easy come easy go' approach can suit cleaners who swap between employers to improve pay or to get the hours they want but it is much more of a problem for live-in workers. Au pairs from outside the EEA, for example, are meant to leave the country within a week if they are not working. Being given very little or no notice about the termination of a contract can therefore cause a crisis which forces them to take any other job that is available. Au pairs are also thrown out on to the street, sometimes in the middle of the night. All the agencies interviewed and the welfare organization that worked with au pairs had stories of au pairs who were just locked out of their employers' home. Sometimes the employer would accuse them of stealing or some other offence but sometimes there would be no explanation at all. Quite often the only people an au pair knows in Britain will be other au pairs, who may not be allowed to have a friend to stay even if she is in dire need. Agents often help out, as do teachers from language classes, and offer au pairs a bed for the night or put them in touch with someone who can take them in. But there are no official bodies that au pairs can go to and some are left entirely alone. The organization Kalayaan, which was established to help overseas domestic workers who had escaped abusive employers, has noticed an increase in the numbers of au pairs coming to them for help recently as they have no where else to turn.[6]

Nannies who live in can also face the prospect of losing their home if they are sacked from their job, but they may have better support networks and resources than au pairs. Nannies from Britain might be able to stay with family or friends and those from abroad might have enough money to pay for somewhere to stay. But even in these circumstances being sacked from a job with no notice can cause tremendous difficulties and distress and having no reference from a previous employer can cause on-going problems.

The pay and conditions of domestic workers have improved since Victorian times but perhaps not as much as we would wish or imagine. Some domestic workers are respected professionals whose work is appreciated and fairly remunerated, but many other domestic workers struggle in isolated circumstances with long working hours and little prospect of a break. Employers need to be much more willing to regard domestic work as a job and to give domestic workers the sorts of rights and working conditions that they would want themselves. While it may be inevitable that a nanny has to work long hours to cover the time her employers travel to and from work, it is not inevitable that she has no regular pay rises or that she is expected to work when she is ill. Many of the problems with domestic work that drove women from it at the beginning of the twentieth century are still problems today. Long hours and low pay are possible to address; the more subtle problems of invisibility and low status while sharing a house with your employer are perhaps more intractable.

Homespace or workplace? The difficulties of working at home

The relationship between domestic workers and their employers involves negotiating the use of a common space as well as the organization of pay and work practices. The fact that the employee's workplace is the employer's home creates a wide range of problems for those trying to negotiate its use and it shapes the relationship that emerges between employers and workers. The relationship between live-in domestic workers and their employers does not end with the working day. It is carried over into the employee's free time and casts the domestic employer as employer, landlady and guardian, particularly for younger domestic workers. This unique characteristic of domestic employment, that it takes place in a home, as a home, not a workshop or office, is immensely important to the experiences of domestic workers. The intimacy of the home creates opportunities for intimacy between employer and employee that are sometimes unwelcome and sometimes the greatest thing domestic work has to offer.

Homes are intimate, private spaces, within which care and affection are experienced and the most important and personal possessions are kept.

Homes are protected to keep out strangers and people feel 'invaded' if they are unable to control access to their homes, for example, if they are burgled. For most working people 'home' and 'work' are separate spaces, perhaps dozens of miles apart. When paid work is carried out inside the home a specific space is set apart for it and the house becomes an office or a workshop. The traditional separation between home and work has underpinned assumptions that whatever happens in the home is not work. Women's work, as housewives and as paid domestic workers, has long been seen as inferior: less important, less valuable and generally less like work than anything that takes place outside the home.

These meanings of home – that it is a private, intimate space, a space that is defined in opposition to work and as a place of belonging – shape the relationships that take place there. Events within the home are emotionally charged, they touch us more deeply than things that happen elsewhere, and this is the context within which domestic work takes place. This emotional charge makes employers and domestic workers highly sensitive to each other's behaviour whether they live in or out. It means that employers can be intolerant and demanding, wanting domestic workers whom they like perhaps more than workers who are good at their job. For domestic workers who live in, the opportunities for conflict are multiplied. Employers can control almost every aspect of their employees' lives: what they eat, whom they see, when they sleep and where they can go in their time off. Living in also allows employers to make huge demands on workers for extra work, because they are 'part of the family'.[7]

Intimacy and invasion: cleaners and their employers

Most people who employ a cleaner could do the work the cleaner does themselves, particularly if everyone in the household pulled their weight. Given that having a cleaner is a choice, it seems strange that, once people have made that choice, they seem not to like the arrangement very much. While some employers kept the same cleaner for years, praised her ability and really appreciated her work, more seemed to resent their cleaners. They criticized their work, dreaded the day they came and would sack cleaners after a relatively short time. These employers seem to be transferring to their cleaners the low value society puts on domestic work generally. By deciding they are too busy or important to do housework, they necessarily have to imagine their cleaners as less important, perhaps less valuable and therefore appropriate, people to clean up after them. These employers seem to find it difficult to negotiate a relationship that they are comfortable with, and this is not surprising. How do you reconcile denigrating someone's work and abilities with having them in your home?

One aspect of the uncomfortable relationship between cleaners and their employers was that both felt cleaning to be intrusive. Employers said they felt 'invaded' by their cleaners and cleaners said that they felt they invaded their employer's privacy. As one put it, 'I make them feel a bit out of place in their own homes.' This intrusion can be deeply felt because it happens in the employer's home, that space over which we are meant to be sovereign, the 'Englishman's castle'.

Working in someone's house also involves the cleaner in becoming privy to information about them, knowing their habits and becoming familiar with most of their possessions. A cleaner may well know better than anyone else how old the household appliances are, where valuables are kept, who puts their dirty socks in the laundry and whether anyone in the family ever cleans the toilet. The cleaner is intimate with the workings of the house but is not intimate with any member of it. As one employer commented:

> Here is this woman who comes in twice a week and in some ways knows much more intimate details about my life than other people and yet I really don't know her at all and we don't communicate. And yes, I don't really sit down over a cup of tea with my cleaner and discuss the events of the day.

This contradiction between closeness and distance is further complicated when employers' attitudes towards their cleaners are taken into account. Some employers develop lasting relationships with their cleaners, come to know about their families and care about them as people. Others are left with the awkward awareness that someone whom they imagine to be somehow inferior to them and their family knows every detail about how they live.

Employers countered the closeness that was created by their cleaner's place in their life in practical and psychological ways. Practical efforts generally focused on avoiding their cleaner whenever possible, even if that meant making life a little more difficult for themselves. Distance could be more completely achieved by sacking a cleaner who appeared to be getting too friendly or who behaved in some other way that made the employer uncomfortable. Some employers had sacked cleaners who wanted to talk to them and some had sacked cleaners whom they didn't like as people.

These decisions had had nothing to do with how good the cleaner was at her job: they were entirely about the employers trying to make themselves feel more comfortable with their cleaners. Having a cleaner whom they personally liked or who would keep her distance from them was what was most important. These employers were prepared to behave in an entirely unfair way, sacking a cleaner for a reason that had nothing to do with her work, in order to try and feel better about the arrangement themselves.

The closeness that is created by sharing space with their domestic employees has long made employers seek to distance themselves from servants in symbolic ways. Traditionally the insistence on uniforms, even when domestic workers were outside the house, use of specific names and physical divisions such as eating separately, served to mark servants as 'other' to the family.[8] Today few employers have means such as uniforms to differentiate themselves from employees but they can create psychological distance between themselves and their cleaners by imagining their cleaner to be different from them in some important way. One of the significant ways in which this was done by the employers I interviewed was by focusing on the nationality or ethnicity of their cleaner. Employers I spoke to all told me the nationality of their cleaner, often mentioning this before any other, perhaps more obviously relevant, fact. These employers seemed to want to stress the characteristics of their cleaners that were the most removed from themselves. An example of how this operated was that *all* the employers who had a cleaner who was not English or Irish said that their cleaner did not speak very good English. Some of these cleaners had been working and living in London for decades and one, from the Philippines, had spoken English all her life. Employers seemed to see a lack of language skills as a justification for their cleaner's role, an external fact that showed how different their cleaner was from them and that legitimated her relative poverty and subsequent need to do cleaning work. None of the employers said how *good* her cleaner's English was, given that it was a second or third language and none of these employers saw her cleaner's lack of language skills as a result of working in a sector that involves isolation and little chance for contact with native speakers, rather than a cause of it.

Employers' focus on their cleaners' language skills hinted at a desire to show that there was something important lacking in their cleaners that explained why they were appropriate domestic workers while they, the employers, were fundamentally different and therefore, not expected to do demeaning work. None of these employers would say that her cleaner was too stupid to do anything except cleaning, and none would say it was 'her place' to clean up after her 'betters', as a Victorian employer might have done. But these employers did want to rationalize the order of things and to comfort themselves that there was something tangible that separated them from their cleaners, a difference that was incontrovertible and enduring.

The stresses and strains of living in

If just sharing space in which a cleaner does her work can cause such complicated relationships between domestic workers and employers, how much more involved are these relationships when domestic workers live in?

Having a domestic worker permanently in the house means that employers have to think of ways to organize sharing space, meals and having visitors as well as organizing work. Domestic workers who live in are subject to two distinct disadvantages over workers with jobs that they can leave at the end of the day. One is that their employers are able to make rules about almost all aspects of their lives, including those aspects that have nothing to do with the performance of their work. The second is that the demands that can be made on them can increase almost infinitely because they are physically present and because they can be integrated into their employer's family and feel obliged to 'help out'.

Domestic workers who are well paid or work in large, formal households are most likely to have self-contained accommodation. This gives them the greatest independence and control over their life outside work but their employers can still apply rules about things such as having friends to stay or having partners. Domestic workers who live more directly in their employers' homes are likely to be in much more direct contact with the family and to have to live in a way that inconveniences their employer as little as possible. Even employers who see accommodation as a substantial part of the remuneration of domestic workers impose rules about how space is used. Employers seem to apply rules that are much more intrusive than those that would be given to a lodger, whilst simultaneously counting the value of lodging as if it were being rented to someone without those restrictions.

Live-in domestic workers have to find a way of sharing space with their employers in as smooth a way as possible. Most of the people interviewed said they did this by being unobtrusive, keeping out of the way in their rooms or going out in their time off if they knew their employer would be in. Domestic workers live in a situation that pervades all aspects of their lives. They have somewhere to live but they do not have a home that is a refuge from the stresses of work, or a place where they are cared for and comforted. Yes, they have somewhere to stay, sometimes somewhere that is much more comfortable than they could hope to afford, but they are also homeless in the sense that they don't really have anywhere where they can relax and be themselves. As one au pair described it:

> I don't really feel like it's my house, I wouldn't say so. That's one of the things which I guess no one really likes with au pair work, because you don't feel comfortable just taking friends home . . . you have to think about what the family wants all the time and is this okay and is that okay and am I doing the right thing? Usually you go out to work and then you go home, but then [with au pairing] you live with the boss all the time.

Food and eating arrangements

One of the things that really shapes relationships between live-in domestic workers and their employers is food – both how meal times are organized and what foods are eaten. As one employer, explained, a woman who had had au pairs in the past but now rejoiced in the fact that she didn't, food is a point where the nitty gritty of relationships is negotiated and where you discover what you really think of other people:

> They eat your Haagen Das ice cream instead of the crap you got the children which you were expecting them to eat and I tell you it's a huge stickler . . . When they would dare eat the smoked salmon it's very tricky. You can't say 'How dare you eat the smoked salmon?' But you want to say, 'How dare you eat the smoked salmon!'

As this quote suggests, arranging food and meal times can lead employers to discover their own feelings about having another person in the house as well as communicating those feelings to the domestic worker. Eating arrangements offer the opportunity to bring a domestic worker into the family, treat her as an equal and extend warmth and generosity to her. They also give employers a chance to make it clear to domestic workers that they are 'staff' not family. Arrangements about food offer both sides the opportunity to clash and miscommunicate repeatedly.

Eating together can reveal differences in expectations and can expose the gulf that exists between two very different groups trying to share a house together. Mila, an au pair from the Slovak Republic, told a story about something that had happened in her first au pair position. She was new to England and she took a job with a Jewish vegetarian family in Hertfordshire:

> They were vegetarians but it didn't matter to me, but the problem was I wasn't told that I can't eat any meat and because I am Catholic and I don't know much about other religions, and I wasn't told I couldn't eat any meat in their house. So, after about one month I bought ham but I brought it with me and I left it in the fridge and then, well I didn't know. So there was a big argument, they were kind of shouting at me. The lady was very, very upset and was shouting 'I don't want this on my plate, I don't want it in my fridge, I don't want this eaten in my house.' So I had to go outside and eat all the ham and I had bought the bigger packet because it was better value and I didn't have much money – I had thirty-five pounds a week – not so much to buy. So I had to eat it, everything at the same time and after that I was sick.

This moving story reveals the mismatch in assumptions and problems with communication that can confound relationships between live-in domestic workers and employers. One can imagine Mila's complete astonishment that a packet of ham could cause so much trouble and her employer's dismay that someone would chose ham, of all things, to bring into a Jewish vegetarian house.

Pam Taylor has described how the practice of servants and 'family' eating separately was an important way in which servants were kept in 'their place' historically. Even in the smallest households a single servant was expected to eat alone. Pam Taylor quotes an interviewee who lived for many years looking after just one other person. They were the only two occupants of the house but always ate separately except during the war when they ate together to save heating two rooms.[9] One has to presume that after the war they went back to their separate meals. The organization of meals is just as important in defining relationships today. Live-in domestic workers can be expected to eat alone, to eat with the whole family or to eat with the children of the family if the parents and children eat at different times. My research with au pairs suggested that few au pairs were welcome to eat with the parents if they had meals without the children and few were given a choice in how their meals were organized.

Eating with someone can imply equal standing and friendliness and one au pair employer explained to me that for her it was a crucial part of the relationship, something that demonstrated equality. She illustrated this by describing something that had happened to a relative:

> My sister in law just got a new au pair and she says she will never sit down at the table with them at mealtimes. She used to potter around the kitchen until eventually my sister in law had a word with her and said, 'You can't do this! You're behaving as though you're my servant. You won't sit down at the table with me. Even if you don't want to have dinner, sit down at the table and have a drink.'

This story highlights that eating arrangements can be important in shaping a relationship, in this case differentiating between 'servant' and 'equal'. It also shows how uncomfortable the employer was when her au pair took a role she did not like, even though it was one that was more subservient than she had wanted. But not all live-in domestic workers, or even all au pairs, are welcome to eat with their employers. One au pair who was interviewed lived in a house that also had a live-in housekeeper and she ate with the housekeeper. When there was a dinner party she was expected to serve guests not to sit down with them.

Some employers behave appallingly towards their au pairs and this can come out in terms of what they expect them to eat. One au pair who was interviewed always ate alone and cooked for herself but was given food by her employer, who was responsible for providing her meals. The employer seems to have resented this and gave the au pair as little as possible. As she described it:

> I was given scraps. It was opened and when they got something new I was given what was left, near the use-by day or sometimes even after that.

An agent who was interviewed had also come across instances of au pairs only being given food that was past its use-by date. These au pairs are not being treated as equally human to their employers. The expectation that au pairs can eat scraps or food that might not be safe resembles a slave/master or human/animal relationship and certainly does not include au pairs as members of the family. Some live-in workers are given no choice in the food they can have or are asked by employers to eat things that are unacceptable to them. Some au pairs who were interviewed said that they used part of their meagre wages to buy food to supplement or replace the food their employers supplied.

Being unseen and unheard[10]

Another way in which live-in domestic workers' lives could be governed by their employers was through the use of rules about how the house was used. Domestic workers could be told not to enter or use certain rooms in the house or only to go in them in order to clean them or to use them if their employers were away. They could also face strict rules about having guests to visit or stay overnight. Rules about visits by male friends or boyfriends were the strictest of all.

Some employers included their domestic workers in the house and encouraged them to join the family watching television in the same way as they might be included in family meal times. Others, perhaps because they had the space to impose divisions, asked or expected their live-in worker to avoid communal spaces. While this might not be organized on the strict 'above stairs' and 'below stairs' lines of the past, it is interesting that many domestic workers were given attic rooms that would originally have been occupied by servants, and lived on a different floor from the rest of the family just as their Victorian and Edwardian predecessors would have done.

Among the au pairs interviewed many were distinctly uncomfortable with using 'family' rooms even if they were not technically banned from them. Some expressed surprise at the very idea when they were asked if they sat in the living room with the family and one au pair explained that the living room in her house was so luxurious, with a portrait of the owner on the wall above the mantelpiece, that she felt far too intimidated to go in there for any reason except to clean. Instead they would stick to their own room and go out of the house whenever they could if the family was in.

Employers exert restrictions over visitors to the house and it can seem reasonable for a householder to have control over who comes and goes in their home. However, these rules can make domestic workers isolated and lonely and can deny their rights as independent adults. Twenty-eight per cent of the au pairs surveyed in London said they were not allowed any friends to stay over night and 41 per cent said that they would not be allowed to have a boyfriend or girlfriend to visit or stay. These rules reflect employers' actions to control access to their homes and perhaps to protect their au pairs, who are mostly young women. However well intentioned such rules are, they are also problematic. They show the ways that employers can intervene in every area of their employees' lives because they live in and they deny their employees the status of independent, sexually active adult, just as rules about no 'followers' (the name given to servants' suitors) did in the past. Employers might not want to think about their au pairs' rights in these terms but they do need to consider how reasonable these restrictions are. Studies of other groups of domestic workers have revealed that it is common for employers to ban their domestic workers from receiving guests, particularly sexual partners.[11]

Exploitation and overwork

As well as employers' ability to intervene in almost any aspect of their domestic workers' lives, the problem of ever-increasing workloads is pervasive for live-in domestic workers. The combination of physical presence in the home and feeling involved with the family can mean that domestic workers 'help out' well past the time they should be working or they take on tasks which are beyond the housework and childcare they are meant to do. For many domestic workers it is this perpetual availability that really defines the job and that is one of its least attractive aspects. Lisa, an au pair from Germany, summed up that this is what it meant to be an au pair for herself and her friend Anna:

> We say [it's a] life between slavery and luxury . . . Because most of the families, especially in north London, are really, really rich and, yeah, you see the life they lead, which is strange because you come from

other homes, normal homes. And the other thing is the slavery, that they can always call on you and say come on do this and do that.

Both Lisa and Anna were just finishing a year working as au pairs. They described the experience as overwhelmingly positive and thought they would miss it in a few months' time, but in the end, it was the problem of living in and being expected to be everything to the family that they found most difficult to take.

Anna was treated as a friend by her employers, included in meals and evening conversations. She liked them and had fitted in with them very well, but she explained that this positive relationship and the commitment she felt led to her doing extra work whenever it was necessary. As she put it:

> I do all the cleaning, repairing, moving furniture, lots of stuff. I can't even tell you all the things I do because it depends. I mean, if something is broken I don't want to leave it.

Domestic workers who work with children and who become involved with them can find that these relationships also create work. Their regard for the children can mean extra babysitting or taking on extra responsibilities. Working with children they have become attached to can also cause domestic workers to stay in jobs with bad conditions and low pay rather than looking for something new.

As exemplified by Katerina Bose's story of being asked to work when she was ill on her day off, living in the employer's house can also mean that domestic workers are at risk of being given work to do at any time. Another au pair, Lisa, said her employers asked her to help them with breakfast every morning, even on a Saturday, which was her whole day off. They asked her to get up at 9.00 am and help to give the children breakfast, just for an hour or so. On the face of it this doesn't seem like much. Lisa is already in the house and 9 is not exceptionally early. But, as she explained, it meant that if she went out on a Friday night, she could not have a lie in, and she could not get up and go out early on Saturday if she wanted to visit another part of the country. Katerina faced a similar problem in that she was asked to clean the kitchen after her employers had had supper every day. She said this meant she could never go away for a weekend, even if she had nothing else to do, and if she got home late on a Saturday evening there was always a pile of dishes waiting for her. She explained:

> There isn't [a curfew] but I have to clean the kitchen, so imagine if I came in at three o'clock and had to clean the kitchen until four

o'clock! I have to think. Sometimes it happens that they are out to dinner then I don't have to come home at all because I am off in the morning so it is up to me. But if they are not out for dinner then I have to, I almost have to think that I will have to work so it's a little bit spoiled. . . . For example, three weeks ago I was in Salisbury. It was such a beautiful trip I enjoyed it so much and I came back, I don't know at eleven, and everything was spoiled by the fact that I had to go straight away into the kitchen and clear up.

Domestic workers who live out are normally saved from having to do these 'little bits' of work at each end of the day that seem to employers to be no trouble at all yet which actually prevent domestic workers from having a whole day off or from using their time as they want to.

The development of emotional ties between domestic workers and employers not only means that workers' responsibilities can be extended beyond their working day but also makes domestic workers less likely to complain. Living in can make discussions difficult because of fears about creating bad feeling. Au pairs and other domestic workers interviewed tended not to complain about extra work and would think of leaving an employer rather than negotiating a workload, in order to keep a pleasant atmosphere.

Ultimately live-in work can be all-consuming and domestic workers' lives can be swallowed by their employers. Employers can prevent domestic workers seeing friends, stop them using the telephone and get offended if they spend time outside the house. Employers can do this because they want to have complete control over their employees and they want domestic workers to be available to work long hours or they fear what their workers will say about them. They can also do it because they can think of no other way of negotiating a relationship within their house and they treat domestic workers like children, albeit children who will never be allowed to grow up and leave home. Connie Mayhew came to England from the Philippines in 1972 to work for a family in London. She was earning just £8 per week. She stayed with them for nine years without a pay rise and described what they were like:

They were quite nice, they were like my parents, but at the end of the day they don't want me to get married. Or [my] day off was half a Wednesday and some Saturdays but then they don't want me to go out, you know and stay in with them and have some supper with them. I think 'that's no life, I'm still young.' They treated me like a daughter, you know. Because they don't have a daughter, they've only got one son . . . but they never put the wages up you know . . . But I didn't mind because I haven't got any more parents to send some money so all the money just for me . . . They also let me learn how to drive and things like that and they send me to English school because my English is not that good . . . In the end they are giving me more [money] but what I really want is some leave.

Connie's employers swallowed her into their family and treated her like a child. They obviously liked her and tried to give her things that they thought she would need but ultimately they could not accept that working for them was her job not her life.

Domestic workers like Connie live a life trapped between luxury and slavery. She was included in a well-off family, much richer than the one she had left behind, but this inclusion enslaved her, robbing her of freedom and choice. Domestic work has many such contradictions. Domestic workers can be poorly paid and unappreciated but they can also be close to their employers and emotionally attached to their families. These contradictions mean that domestic work is different from most other jobs and opportunities for domestic workers to be mistreated are ever present.

However, as the next chapter shows, the problems with domestic work do not have to be taken for granted, they can be addressed. The working conditions of domestic workers can be improved and the sector professionalized. We can also start tackling the inequalities that cause some people to become domestic workers and others to become employers. Then we can solve the problems more permanently.

7 | Conclusion
Solving the servant problem

This chapter looks at what needs to be done about the growth in paid domestic employment. It looks at ways that the domestic employment sector could be improved and at how domestic employment could be ended. It begins by considering some possible small-scale changes that could be made by domestic workers, employers and the government that would improve people's experiences and make domestic workers and employers less vulnerable to each other. These include measures such as unionization, professionalization and an improved role for regulated agencies to monitor workloads and pass on information from the government.

The chapter then looks at the broader-scale social changes that would be necessary to deal with our current 'servant problem'. These include tackling the global-scale and more local-scale income inequalities, gender inequalities and the ways in which work and home life are organized. All these trends underpin domestic employment and none of them is a thing to be proud of as a society or makes the lives of the majority any better. Improving the working conditions of domestic workers and challenging broader-scale problems are not 'either/or' choices. Working conditions within the sector need to be improved and the inequalities that feed domestic employment need to be addressed. Both things will make life better for those in greatest need and confronting the social inequalities that underpin domestic employment will make life better for the vast majority of people.

Improving the sector

The majority of domestic workers in Britain today may be treated better than their counterparts of a hundred years ago, but there is still much that could be done to improve the sector and to make pay and working conditions amongst domestic workers more akin to those of other employees. Domestic workers themselves, their employers and government could all act to make domestic employment more stable, more fairly recompensed and more professional.

Domestic workers: the need for organization

Domestic workers have traditionally lacked the labour organizations that have helped other group of workers improve their pay and conditions. Unionization has been very problematic for domestic workers but it is not impossible and there are examples in many parts of the world of groups who have organized. These organizations of domestic workers have been important in preventing some of the worst abuses by employers and in tackling more commonplace issues of pay and conditions. A union or other organization could work to raise standards in the sector generally and to professionalize domestic workers. This could be in the interests of employers as well as the workers themselves.

Domestic workers are a notoriously difficult group to organize because of their isolation in separate houses. This presents practical problems because domestic workers do not necessarily know each other or meet up as a group, and they may not have the same time off or be able to travel far to meetings. Working inside a family home can also mean that domestic workers identify with their employers and overlook their own rights. Pam Taylor has commented on the fact that domestic service in the inter-war years could be thought of as a 'total institution' where all aspects of behaviour are controlled and where it is difficult not to accept the role defined for you.[1] The same is true for some domestic workers today, particularly those who live in and have little contact with people outside their employer's family. Even employers' efforts at kindness in including domestic workers as part of the family can enforce the totality of a worker's definition by her job.

Domestic workers, however, do resist. They can do this as individuals by refusing to accept definitions of themselves as 'just a cleaner' or 'just an au pair'. They can get support and solidarity from meeting other domestic workers informally and swapping stories or getting advice, and they can do it in more formal, campaigning organizations.

Studies from all over the world have documented the way that informal gatherings of domestic workers develop in cities where they are employed.[2] These might be at specific churches, in parks where they take children to play or just in public squares. For migrant workers these gatherings can offer the chance to hear news from home, see friends or relatives and eat familiar foods. For all workers they offer the opportunity to hear about other people's pay and working conditions, to find out if there are new jobs going and generally to feel part of a group. Such friendship, support and practical advice can be invaluable in helping domestic workers cope with their isolation and in ensuring that they do not accept the worst pay or work arrangements. For au pairs in Britain, English language classes can provide a similar forum. Au pairs can make friends, discuss their experiences and reflect on how fair their treatment is. The teachers at language schools can also become very knowledgeable about the treatment of au pairs and can be useful sources of advice and support.

Formal unions have also been organized in many different countries. In Latin America, for example, where domestic employment is very widespread, there are unions in many individual countries and a Latin America-wide domestic workers' organization. These campaign to improve domestic workers' rights and operate to help individual workers find new jobs so they can leave the worst employers.[3] In other parts of the world smaller and less formalized organizations have helped domestic workers by ending their isolation and giving them the support of colleagues.

In Britain the Professional Association of Nursery Nurses, a section of the Professional Association of Teachers, represents nannies and campaigns over pay and conditions. It will represent members with a problem, but it does not believe in striking or other forms of industrial action and only has about 5,500 members, which includes nursery nurses in nurseries as well as nannies.[4]

Another group of domestic workers in Britain who have organized successfully are overseas domestic workers who became undocumented after leaving abusive employers. These workers have organized in some of the most difficult circumstances to campaign against the concession in the immigration rules that created their situation. A group of undocumented workers, originally from the Philippines, but then including people from many other countries, formed the group 'Waling Waling', named after a flower that grows in the mountains in the Philippines and is found under rocks rather than out in the open. They worked to support members of the group in all aspects of their lives, organizing social events and outings as well as campaigning politically. Waling Waling was supported in its campaign by a group called Kalayaan (meaning 'freedom' in Tagalog). Members of the public who supported the domestic workers' campaign formed Kalayaan and were able to be the public face of the campaign, working with the media and lobbying politicians. The undocumented status of Waling Waling members meant that this was impossible or dangerous for them. Waling Waling also worked with the Transport and General Workers' Union, which allowed them to become members. This gave the group strong institutional support and helped draw attention to their situation. The campaign against the concession to the immigration rules has been largely successful and the law has been changed as a result. Waling Waling is now the United Workers' Association, a broader group with links to domestic workers throughout Europe, through the 'Respect' network.[5]

The success of Waling Waling and Kalayaan shows that it is possible for domestic workers to organize in even the most precarious situations and that such organizations can make real strides in tackling injustice. A broader organization of British domestic workers is possible and it could make a real difference to everyone working in the sector. A well-represented and formally organized union could also be beneficial to employers. It could work to raise standards throughout the sector and could disseminate good practice to domestic workers. It could also offer a forum where disputes could be resolved and could offer employers help and advice in organizing the domestic help they want successfully. Unions are recognized in many industries as playing an invaluable part in negotiating for better working practices and for protecting workers from low wages, long hours and dangerous working conditions. There is no reason why domestic workers should not have the same protection and the ability to campaign around issues that they identify as important.

The role of employers

Domestic workers' conditions could be improved by organizing to establish a more professional standing. Employers could aid this by taking their role more seriously, too. One thing that few people consider when they take on domestic workers is that they will be their *employer*, their *manager* and they may not really know how to go about doing that. Taking on a nanny or a part-time cleaner may not be the same as running a multi-national company but it does still involve important management skills. The nature of domestic work, its content and location can mean that it is a particularly delicate relationship to manage. Few employers think in advance about how they are going to manage domestic workers, what possible problems might arise and how those could best be solved. In fact, many employers forget that their domestic worker is doing is a job at all. As a result, unsurprisingly, lots of employers are very bad managers.

There are a number of reasons why it is so easy for employers to neglect their role or to fail to realize that domestic work is work. First, they may have very little contact with their domestic worker and exercise no direct control over her work. Someone who has a cleaner coming in once a week at a time when they are not there is unlikely to see themselves as managing that person's labour. Second, people managing full-time or live-in domestic workers may be preoccupied with the issues attached to having someone in their home and so overlook the work-based part of their relationship. For example, au pair employing families are encouraged by Home Office rhetoric to be 'hosts' to a family member rather than employers, and these families might thus prioritize developing this relationship. Lastly, the long-standing separation between 'work' and 'home' together with ingrained assumptions that all women know how to do housework and childcare mean that domestic labour is not thought of as work and employers presume that any woman they employ will be able to do the job.

All this means that basic good principles and practice of employing someone or managing them get forgotten. Domestic employers quite often don't realize they need to think about their employee's rights as well as considering the best ways to help them do their job. Bridget Anderson found that in a survey of nearly 200 employers in four countries that 48 per cent did not think domestic workers had a right to a contract, 70 per cent thought domestic workers should not be able to join unions, 52 per cent thought they should not have the right to minimum wage and 45 per cent thought domestic workers should not have any fixed hours of employment. As a result of these sorts of attitudes we see domestic workers who get no holiday entitlement, are sacked if they are ill, never get their pay increased or have many hours of their work considered as a 'favour' rather than recompensed as overtime.

Telling it like it is: the need for communication

Communication between domestic workers and employers often seems to be lacking. This seems strange when you think of them as often working and living so closely together, but this very intimacy can cause problems. Poor communication can lead to domestic workers not knowing what is expected of them or whether they are doing a good job. It can also mean that they get sacked when they have done nothing wrong and thus they are given no chance to change their behaviour.

Employers also seem to be very bad at communicating. This can begin with simple things like not telling a domestic worker what they want them to do, perhaps because employers assume that all housework is the same and their domestic worker will just know how to get on. Katerina Bose, one of the au pairs interviewed, told a story about a friend of hers who arrived at a new au pair job to be met by the mother in the family at the door and told, 'Go to your room. I'm sorry, I don't feel well.' Katerina continued:

> She didn't even show her where her room is, so she looked for her own room in the house and was sitting there for four hours. She didn't know what to do. Then the lady told the son of the family to tell her that she should prepare dinner for the whole family. She came into the

kitchen, she didn't know what to cook because the fridge was empty. Can you imagine for the first time in the foreign kitchen, you don't know where things are, what to do, what you are allowed to?

This may be quite an extreme situation, but Katerina continued to explain that lots of the au pairs she knew commented on how little they are told about what is expected of them. She reflected on her own experience with her current employers, where she works in a very large house, quite different from any home she had lived in before.

> You come and they don't tell you exactly what you should do. If I had an au pair, and I don't want to have any, but if I had, I would write it down for her, everything, clearly, what she shall do, everything, systematically. But they just accept you, they tell you very superficially, like 'cleaning', but they don't, show you. If [the housekeeper] wasn't there, I'd be lost. She told me, I always remember the first day, I listened to everything, I ran up to my room and wrote down everything and in the evening I had a paper full of various notices and I had to create some kind of system. I really can't understand why they aren't able to do it.

This lack of clear communication can cause real problems. Domestic workers never know if they are doing the right things, too much work or too little and they therefore suffer unnecessary anxiety. Employers run the risk of not having the work done as they would want it – either different tasks are done, or jobs aren't done in the way they like. Employers might be quite vague or unsure of what they want done before a domestic worker starts, but the problem is that, if they then don't like what is done, they are much less unsure that they are unhappy about it.

If a problem does arise with how a domestic worker does her work employers can be very bad at dealing with it. Some employers do identify what the problem is, think about what they want to be different or how a practice could be changed and then talk to their employee about it. Others, however, feel awkward criticizing someone else and either put up with the problem or sack the worker, making some excuse so they don't feel that they are being rude. The first situation is unhelpful, the second is downright outrageous. Yes, telling someone that there is a problem is uncomfortable; yes it is an unpleasant situation; but, unfortunately, if you want to employ someone it comes with the territory, and managing that awkwardness is the employer's responsibility. In large organizations managers sometimes argue that their higher pay is recognition of some of the disagreeable situations they have to deal with and the responsibility they have to take. In a domestic setting there is no compensation for doing this but it still may need to be done.

If an employer puts up with a situation they are unhappy with two things can happen. One is that the person they employ never has the chance to improve because they don't know that there is a problem. The other is that the employer will moan about the domestic worker behind her back, criticize her to their friends and generally feel dissatisfied. In an industry where jobs are found by word of mouth this could be quite damaging. It can also mean that the employer becomes resentful and is reluctant to give pay rises or time off, all because *they* have not dealt with a problem.

If an employer sacks a domestic worker without telling her there is a problem or giving her a chance to improve, no one could argue they are behaving fairly. The situation could easily exist where a live-in domestic worker is given no guidance about what she is to do, uses her best efforts to imagine what her duties are and then is sacked and made homeless by her employer without any discussion. This kind of treatment, where domestic workers are dismissed because their employers feel too embarrassed to discuss problems, is not at all uncommon. A number of employers I interviewed said it was how they dealt with tricky situations. Their stories revealed that they did not do this to be cruel; in fact, their accounts revealed that they felt themselves to be victims, 'nice' people, not tough enough to deal with being rude to someone and trying to save face all around. However, in practice, getting rid of a domestic worker if they do not work in quite the desired way and then replacing them with someone else is to treat that person as if they are disposable. Such domestic workers are not being treated like employees – they are just thrown away when their employers decide they aren't quite right.

Discussions with employers about how they envisaged the 'perfect' domestic worker revealed the extent to which employers are silent about their expectations and the impact this can have for domestic workers. I asked employers what they most liked and disliked in domestic workers and how they imagined the perfect domestic worker to be. Replies revealed that all employers wanted domestic workers who were honest and reliable. Beyond that, however, there was little agreement about which characteristics were favourable and which were not. People who employed nannies or au pairs said that they wanted someone who was good with children but only one person employing a cleaner said that they wanted someone who was good at cleaning! One example of quite disparate expectations was to do with how much independence cleaners should exercise. Some employers said that they wanted a cleaner with 'initiative', someone who would look at what needed doing and get on with it. Other employers said quite the opposite, that they would feel invaded if they came home and discovered a cleaner had turned out the cupboards without talking to them. Both groups described the type of cleaner they wanted as a 'good' cleaner and her opposite as 'bad'; some had sacked cleaners in the past for having too much or too little initiative, yet none of these employers would have articulated this preference in seeking out a cleaner. Both groups assumed that their preference was universal and a 'good' cleaner would just be that way, despite the fact that it would be a sacking offence in some other jobs! It is hardly surprising if employers are unhappy with cleaners if mind-reading skills are actually more important than cleaning skills.

Guilty Secrets

Another hugely important influence on the way that employers manage domestic workers, and another reason why they often do it so badly, is guilt. Employers who do not take it for granted that they will employ help feel guilty about not doing the work themselves. They feel guilty about being able to afford to pay someone else to do it; if they think of themselves as feminists they may feel guilty about employing another woman; and if they are employing childcare they feel guilty about leaving their children. Those employers who really like not having to do all their own domestic work can also feel guilty about that, too.

The roots of this guilt are incredibly deep, based in social expectations about women's responsibilities for their families and in Dickensian images of bloated, lazy masters and starving, overworked servants. Numerous studies have shown the anguish many women suffer when leaving their children and going to work. The assumption that mothers, not fathers or families, are responsible for raising children is pervasive. Media reports about abandoned 'latch key kids' running riot or not achieving at school all add to the guilt women feel if they go out to work. Some women also feel guilt about not doing all the housework in their homes. Many women are brought up to believe that their role is to look after their family and to maintain the home they live in. They don't really expect the men they live with, or anyone else, to do any housework. Perhaps even more women have ambivalent feelings about their responsibility for housework. They don't really see why they should do everything at home but they know that society generally does judge them, and not the rest of the family, on the state of their house. Precisely because housework is done in private most people know very little about what other people do: how long they spend, what corners they cut, what lengths they go to, what they clean and what they overlook. This can leave women with a nagging feeling that everyone else is coping better than they are and again leaves them feeling guilty or inadequate if they employ help.

Employers who have left-wing leanings can feel guilty about employing someone else, and women can feel particularly guilty about passing their most hated chores on to another woman. Lots of people do not want to be 'the kind of person' who employs domestic help. They don't want to think of themselves as privileged or lazy and they don't like the idea that they can easily afford to pay someone else to do things they don't want to do. As a friend put it to me when explaining why employing a cleaner is so uncomfortable:

> I would always be thinking that she would think that I thought I was better than her and that's why I didn't do my cleaning and she did. But I'm not like that. I don't think like that and I would want her to know, but, well, that's why it doesn't work.

All this guilt then feeds back into the relationships people develop with the domestic workers they employ, who become entangled in their feelings about work, home and housework. Guilt means that employers of domestic workers have much more complicated feelings about their position than employers in other situations and this tends to stop them wanting to take on the role in a straightforward way. Guilt-ridden employers can seek to overcome their feelings by trying to be 'friends' with their domestic workers. One study of nanny employers[6] who worked outside the home suggested that they develop 'false kin' relationships with their nannies, whereby the nanny is considered by the employer to be like a sister or an older daughter. These feelings result from the gratitude women feel towards their nannies for allowing them to combine work and motherhood. The extensive guilt these mothers feel about leaving their children is converted into deep regard for the person who enables them to get on with their life.

While being friendly towards employees might sound nice it can be highly problematic. In the first place, domestic workers may not be looking for new friends and employers' efforts in this direction can be intrusive rather than welcome. Second, employers who want to be friendly can treat domestic workers in inappropriate ways. They may give workers presents rather than recognizing their rights. So at Christmas they might give their cleaner a gift rather than a cash bonus that would be more welcome. They can overlook that the extra hours spent babysitting is work for the employee rather than a favour from a friend. Employers can also react to domestic workers' behaviour in unsuitable ways if they are trying to establish a warm rather than a professional relationship. These employers can give priority to selecting domestic workers they like and can sack workers they don't get on with or criticize workers who don't reciprocate their efforts at friendliness. Interestingly, in her survey of 200 employers, Bridget

Anderson found that those who described their relationship with their domestic worker as 'friendly and professional' have lower expectations of the rights of domestic workers – such as days off or holiday pay – than those who described the relationship as just professional or just friendly.[7]

So one simple improvement that could be made in the functioning of the domestic employment sector is for employers to take their role seriously – to find out what their responsibilities are and to behave in a professional manner. This doesn't mean being distant or unfriendly but it does mean thinking about how they would want to be treated in a job and trying to apply some of the same principles. Domestic employers, like employers in any other situation, have responsibilities towards the people they employ. They should take seriously their long-term welfare and their current ability to do their job effectively without stress or anxiety. Employers need to be clear about what is due to their employees and should not think of themselves as generous if they do just more than the bare minimum. They need to consider the way they communicate and find ways to do this in an appropriate manner. Employers should also look at 'the baggage' that they bring into the relationships they have with their domestic workers. They need to be honest about their behaviour and make efforts to behave fairly at all times. All this might make employing someone a bit more expensive or a bit more time-consuming, but is being treated as if your job is a job really so much to ask?

To regulate or not to regulate

Domestic employment seems to be crying out for some kind of government intervention or effective regulation. The problems that domestic workers face in terms of extended hours, lack of holidays, low pay or unfair dismissal appear to be the result of the informal and unrecognized nature of their work. Much could be done to improve their rights and to make domestic workers and their employers aware of those rights. But even with improved legal protection, the fact that domestic workers are hidden in private homes makes enforcing any guidance difficult or impossible. This means that a broader and more imaginative approach needs to be taken if efforts to improve conditions for domestic workers are going to be effective. What needs to be addressed is the dependence of domestic workers on their employers, a dependence which disempowers the workers and gives employers completely disproportionate control over their lives. Ultimately, a more professionalized and independent domestic work force that has improved pay and working conditions could be better for employers, too.

There are lots of bad employers in lots of sectors of the economy; they are not unique to the domestic setting. What makes the situation of domestic workers unusual is the amount of control employers can exert. Such workers can also become absorbed into their employers' lives emotionally and will do more work than they are paid for, or not ask for pay rises because they want to feel like part of the family. This is obviously a particular problem for live-in domestic workers but it can also affect those who live out if they work for one employer or stay with an employer for a long time.

Domestic workers can be especially vulnerable if their own legal standing is compromised in some way. The case of overseas domestic workers in Britain illustrates the worst-case scenario if domestic workers are not legally able to leave abusive employers. Other migrant domestic workers are in a weak position because they are undocumented or have had their migration sponsored by a specific employer, as happens in the United States. Even part-time cleaners who are working while claiming benefits are susceptible to employers ignoring their rights because they are not in a position to enforce them. The first step for these domestic workers is to ensure that their legal status is improved so that they are not trapped in abusive or unfair working conditions. This means making it easier for migrants to work legally or to change their employer and it means seriously addressing the barriers that benefit-dependent women face when trying to enter formal sector work.

These are obviously large steps but they are not impossible ones. There are some smaller changes that could be made that might also improve the working arrangements of domestic workers and protect them from the worst employers. Much more could be done by government to make sure that both employers and domestic workers are aware of their rights and of best practice in domestic employment. A small number of publications exist which do give guidance on employing a nanny or au pair, and a range of web sites offer advice to people thinking of employing childcare in their homes. However, there is less specific guidance available on being a *good* employer and very little is done to ensure that domestic workers know their rights.

Employment agencies

Domestic employment agencies could be invaluable in this role. Good agencies are the real specialists in the domestic labour sector – they know about work practices, about common problems and they hear about things from both the domestic worker's and employer's point of view. However, not all agencies are good and, as they are not licensed or regulated in any way, it is more difficult for the government to use them to gather and disseminate information. The regulation of domestic agencies may be a necessary step to improving working conditions for domestic workers and to offering some reassurance to employers (particularly those who will be leaving children alone with a domestic worker).

Anyone can set up a domestic employment agency and take responsibility for placing workers in other people's homes. As agencies are not registered, they are not inspected and very large numbers of them come and go all the time. Inevitably there are agencies that have no compunction about placing domestic workers in illegal or dangerous situations and who will place workers who do not have the required references or experience. They want to be paid their arrangement fee and do not really care how they earn it. One day I was interviewing an agent who placed au pairs in South London. She received a call from a prospective client. She talked to the client briefly and then said she would not be able to help. Afterwards she told me that the caller had said she had a six-month-old baby and would soon be returning to work. She was looking for a 'live-out au pair' to work for about 40 hours a week doing housework and some childcare and was thinking of paying about £40 per week. I expressed surprise and outrage that someone should even suggest such an arrangement but the agent said, 'She'll phone around a few more places and someone will find her what she wants. I won't do it, but someone else will.' Internet sites are also testament to how happy some agencies are to work outside the law. A quick glance over sites offering to place workers, particularly au pairs, shows agencies offering 'mature' au pairs (i.e. those over 27 and therefore not covered by the au pair agreement), au pairs from countries outside Europe and jobs for au pairs for long hours each week. These sites are easy to find and could be viewed by anyone in authority who took an interest, but the people running them obviously feel quite secure that no one cares enough about domestic workers to stop them.

Good employment agencies do more than just work within the law – they strive to match domestic workers to suitable posts and they give help and advice to make the arrangement as successful as possible. They will discuss what it is reasonable to ask a domestic worker to do and pass on tips that have helped others in the past. They can act as friends to both sides in the relationship and can intervene if disputes arise. Some agencies have been proactive in making sure domestic workers know their rights. They will ensure au pairs have leaflets containing Home Office advice or that nannies know that their tax and National Insurance must be paid. Agencies are a good medium to pass on such advice because they can establish good relationships with domestic workers and employers and are often the first port of call if workers or employers have questions or problems.

The regulation of domestic employment agencies would offer an opportunity to support agencies that are behaving scrupulously and to confront those that are more 'relaxed' in their attitudes towards the law. Regulation would need to involve some sort of registration and this would mean that all agencies placing staff in domestic positions would be known about. Government departments could then disseminate information through them or could use their lists of placements to get information to the people who need it most. Such records would also mean that the location and contractual conditions of many domestic workers could be known, offering them a very basic level of protection. Under such arrangements it would be possible for domestic workers or employers to make complaints about the worst agencies (with the threat that the agency could eventually be shut down) and if workers or employers were known to have behaved irresponsibly their details could be distributed to all agencies so they would not be dealt with again. Such procedures would need to be very carefully designed in order to avoid their abuse, but, given that many other sectors have codes of practice and regulations that businesses adhere to, it should be possible. Of course none of this would help domestic workers who are not placed by agencies but it might work to raise the general standards and expectations within the sector as a whole.

It has recently become possible for nannies to be officially registered and for their work to be inspected by Ofsted. However, there is no pressure on either employers or nannies to enter the scheme unless employers are claiming the childcare element of Working Tax Credit. There are some arguments in favour of inspection for all domestic workers caring for children. Employers can be highly anxious about the quality of care their children are receiving but they are not necessarily qualified or able to judge their carer's work. Inspection could also include checking the safety of the employer's home as a workplace and could offer some basic protection to domestic workers. Such a plan, however, is not without some difficulties. Regular inspections may be appropriate to childcarers who are well trained and could include some aspect of continuing professional development that would be very useful, but surely it would be more appropriate to offer training rather than judgment to unqualified domestic workers, such as au pairs? Then of, course, there are the practical difficulties. Who would fund such a scheme and who would know whether all the necessary people had been registered? Employers who do not want to pay for qualified childcare are unlikely to be prepared to pay for an unqualified au pair or mother's help to be registered. It will be interesting to see how widely the registration of nannies is taken up and what the longer-term outcomes of the scheme are.

Support and recognition

The growth in paid domestic employment has been largely invisible and unrecognized by official or government organizations. This lack of visibility has meant that there are no real resources available to help domestic workers, nor has much effort been made to understand their situation. Two things that could be done to improve the lot of some domestic workers are the provision of funding to welfare organizations that work with domestic workers and a reconsideration of the real role of workers such as au pairs.

Live-in domestic workers, particularly but not only if they are migrants from abroad, can find themselves entirely isolated if they work for an abusive employer. There are a number of groups who work with domestic workers who might be able to help but none of these has adequate resources and most domestic workers would not know about them.

The Home Office has undertaken to provide all domestic workers who enter Britain with their employers information about their legal status and rights. It also produces an advice leaflet for au pairs and has the same information on its web site. However, many domestic workers never see these leaflets and many others fall outside the groups that they cover. The government could do more to work with groups that support domestic workers to publicize the resources that are available to them and to make those resources more robust. As well as possibly helping individuals in dire circumstances, by raising the profile of domestic workers' rights such government action might render employers less likely to behave badly towards any domestic workers.

The government could also usefully reconsider the precise conditions of the au pair scheme and recognize that many au pairs are hard-working employees and not 'family members'. Many people engaged in the scheme, au pairs, host families and agencies, consider the arrangement to be very largely successful and to fulfil needs for both au pairs and employers. However, it is clear that many 'au pairs' are not really taken on in the spirit of cultural exchange and are just used as a cheap form of domestic labour. At the very least the recommended rates of pay for au pairs should be raised and employers should be expected to pay for English language classes in most situations. There are few employers who could not afford such fees relatively easily but for au pairs the costs can be prohibitively high. When au pairs attend language classes they can make friends and develop an all-important support and social network. This is something that should be very strongly encouraged by the Home Office. The advice issued by the Home Office could also give better guidance about what work it is reasonable to expect an au pair to do.

This would not discourage the worst employers but it might help inform people who do want to behave well. Lastly, I would question the appropriateness of the rhetoric of 'family membership' and the language such as 'pocket money' and 'host family' that it includes. This approach seems to deny the very real work that au pairs do and overlooks the true role they have in supporting many British families. If the government does not want young, unqualified people from abroad to be seen as a substantial childcare workforce in Britain it should do more to provide and subsidize other forms of childcare rather than denying the work that is actually done.

I am aware that this section has concentrated on examining ways that domestic workers can be protected from employers and has not addressed some employers' fears about domestic workers abusing their position, for example by stealing or damaging things or, at worst, harming the children in their care. This is because the risks employers pose to domestic workers are of a different order of magnitude to those that employers face themselves. Statistics show that physical and psychological abuse of workers is widespread in situations where employers feel they are unlikely to be detected or punished, whereas there have been only a very small number of cases of domestic workers harming the children in their care. These cases are of course tragic and any efforts that can be made to prevent similar occurrences in the future should be supported. However, it seems that paid carers are less likely to kill or injure their charges than parents are, so they cannot be considered a particular risk.

The Louise Woodward case in the USA did illustrate that training and experience are invaluable for people looking after babies and small children. Perhaps the most reasonable worry parents have is that a young, inexperienced carer will lack the knowledge to create a stimulating environment for their children. Better training and opportunities for continuing professional development would do more to address these fears than any amount of legislation or monitoring.

Other fears that employers have, e.g. that their employees will steal from them or use their belongings, can only really be addressed by developing a relationship of mutual respect and trust. It is not surprising that domestic workers who are paid a pittance by employers who are obviously extremely wealthy become resentful. Fair pay and conditions for staff are probably the best insurance for employers.

Solving the servant problem

There are things that could be done to improve the workings of the domestic employment sector, to protect domestic workers and employers and to make the experience of domestic employment more positive and, perhaps, financially rewarding. However, these are all measures that tinker at the edges of the problem rather than addressing the fundamental and deep-seated inequalities that underpin the growth of domestic employment. It is not reasonable or desirable to create a new Victorian era in the twenty-first century, where the global poor serve the global rich and service their consumption-driven, status-chasing lifestyles. Private, individual solutions to the problems of combining work, family and leisure are not enough. For everyone who buys in help and creates some time for themselves, or finds a way to continue in work while raising children, or manages to present a home they are proud of, there are many hundreds who are not managing, who cannot cope, have no leisure or cannot work. Social, collective solutions are needed that attack the very inequalities between people that feed demand for domestic help. New ways of organizing life and work are also needed that let everyone have both work and life with dignity and even a bit of leisure time. Such changes would deplete the demand for domestic workers and they would make life better for everyone.

Global inequalities

Many of the domestic workers in Britain and the rest of the world have taken on domestic work not out of desire or choice but because of poverty and lack of opportunities in their home countries. Even au pairs, who are generally well educated and European (normally a privileged geographical affiliation) find that they are pushed to become domestic workers in Britain in order that they may learn English to compete in the increasingly globalized job market. The processes that cause poverty for families in the Philippines or that create unemployment in Slovenia are not natural or accidental. The world economy is organized and directed in the interests of those who are already economically powerful. Deliberately designed and implemented policies and actions from the few bring privation and destitution to the many around the world.

Within Britain and other countries, as well as at a global scale, economic processes and political policies underpin the income inequalities that feed demand for domestic help and create people looking for domestic employment. The continuing concentration of wealth in the hands of the richest 5 or 10 per cent of British society is a result of financial deregulation and tax and benefit regimes that have taken from the poor and given to the rich. The global economic situation creates a context within which British governments have acted. The drive to be internationally competitive and 'flexible' results in less security of employment, a pared-back welfare state and a 'business-friendly' tax structure, all things that make it easier for the rich to employ the poor in their homes.

Employers need to think about the way that economic inequalities may be enabling or enhancing their lifestyle. Are they out having an enjoyable dinner because babysitting is provided for free by an au pair? Are they assured of never doing cleaning themselves because foreign domestic workers will always be affordable? Maybe they think they are helping by providing a job for a woman who obviously really needs work. But is that all there is to it? On a small scale, employers need to question whether they employ their domestic workers in such a way that it supports them as much as possible. Do they pay fair, really fair, wages? Do they make sure their domestic worker can access training such as English classes if she wants to? Do they worry about whether the people they employ are managing to maintain links with their families at home – can they call or e-mail easily? Are they given enough holiday and enough pay to see their children or their parents regularly? Employers who are able to take advantage of global economic inequalities to access domestic help must make sure they do not exacerbate those inequalities in the way they organize their employee's work. They must take responsibility for knowing the effects of their choices and they must treat their domestic workers with respect and generosity.

On a grander scale, employers should also take responsibility for thinking about the wider situation that allows them to employ help and should not claim that they are passive actors in an unwanted situation. They should ask themselves whether they would be happy to support new trade or loan arrangements that are less damaging to poorer countries and whether they know about the impacts of the policies they do support on people worse off than themselves. And we probably need to ask whether all domestic employers do just find themselves able to take advantage of an economic order that they did not bring about. The people who run the world, who make decisions about finance, trade and politics and whose actions have real effects on people's livelihoods are probably domestic employers, too. Owners and managers of companies that can move jobs from here to there or negotiate a lower price from a supplier elsewhere, stock brokers who can destroy jobs thousands of miles away as they 'buy, buy' and 'sell, sell' and politicians who adopt punishing welfare regimes to be popular with business, are all actors who perpetuate the inequalities that create domestic workers and employers. There are some people who are responsible for the situation we are in, who benefit directly – and immensely – from the poverty that others suffer. They are not innocent bystanders: they are the people who act to create the unequal world we live in. Income inequalities are at the core of the servant problem, they make it possible for one person to buy the labour of another. We need to understand where those inequalities come from, how they are perpetuated and why they have the effects that they do, before we can begin to tackle them.

Work–life balance

The global economic situation creates an environment of polarized wealth and poverty within which domestic employment can thrive. But there are also smaller-scale and more specific practices that boost demand for domestic workers and that can more easily be tackled. The organization of work, and attitudes towards paid work, are two of these areas and the move towards a real balance between work and life beyond work would be a benefit for employers, domestic workers and society more widely.

Work overwhelms other areas of life both because of its practical organization and because of attitudes that value work over all other activities. The basic practical problem with work for most people is that it takes up too much time. People work longer hours, are expected to work flexibly and to show their commitment by staying later and later at work. People travel more as part of their work and people travel for longer to get to work. Added to the growth in working anti-social hours, work has become something that is not contained in the nine to five. It spills out into the rest of the week, into our houses and the rest of our lives. At the same time alternatives to work have never been so poorly valued. People who are not in paid work, because they are raising families, are disabled or cannot find suitable jobs, are being pushed into the labour market harder than in previous decades. People who are in work are taking on more of it. People are choosing work over leisure and family, as we increasingly define ourselves through our jobs.

The ever-ready, perpetually available worker might seem like a good thing to individual employers, who argue that they need flexibility and commitment from employees to respond to a dynamic and competitive global market, but it is not good for society more generally nor for the people involved or their families. Existing 'work–life balance' policies are welcome but have done nothing to tackle the basic problems of long hours and ways of working that are flexible for employers but inflexible for workers. Much more needs to be done to make work and home life more compatible. This includes measures such as improved rights to parental leave, term-time only working, a reduction in the length of the working week and longer and better-paid maternity and paternity leave. But it also means much more than this: it means that work needs to become a smaller part of our lives, both in terms of the hours we spend on it and in terms of the importance placed on it. Changes in government policy are a first and necessary step towards this.

Improved work–life balance would reduce the need for domestic workers. Shorter and more manageable working hours would make childcare easier to arrange. Having more time outside work would make housework seem like a less onerous task in precious leisure hours. Restructuring work so that it is shared out more fairly between more people could also mean that people who are currently employed in domestic work would have other, better options. They would be able to work at times that fitted with their domestic responsibilities and could enter formal-sector employment with better working conditions and possibilities for training and an end to their isolation.

Childcare

Following directly from this is the need for publicly provided, affordable, flexible childcare. Current government policy, which supports increasing work hours and flexibility, and which hails work as the only route out of poverty, but without really addressing the colossal shortage of affordable childcare, is absolutely unworkable. The National Childcare Strategy has done more than any other policy in the post-war era to increase the supply of childcare places but it has still done nothing like enough. The current UK government is the first to abandon the rhetoric of childcare as the responsibility of mothers, because it wants those mothers in the workforce. But for most families childcare still does fall to women and many of them are now having to combine that traditional responsibility with many more hours of paid work.

Childcare policy needs to reflect the realities of working patterns today, the long hours, unusual shifts, evening, weekend and night working and the push for flexibility. It also needs to recognize the difficulties some people have travelling between home, childcare and work. Childcare needs to be convenient, accessible, affordable and high quality. Parents need to be feel confident about leaving their children and need to have somewhere to do it.

Childcare should also be made available for people to do things other than just work. At the very least, unemployed parents should be entitled to access childcare so that they can develop the networks and confidence that will help them in looking for work. But more than this, childcare should be available so that people can create a little bit of space in their lives, the way that some nanny employers are currently able to. This could be time to do the shopping without a screaming toddler, time to go to the dentist or take the car to be serviced, or just time to feel sane. Having childcare that offered parents the chance to leave their children for even just a little bit longer than their working day would make a huge difference.

Good quality, widespread, socialized childcare would be a more efficient way of looking after children than the use of individual nannies or au pairs. It would create the opportunity to offer childcare staff improved pay and conditions, provide recognition of their skills and create a more professionalized career structure. Socially provided, subsidized childcare would also break the link between the cost of care to parents and the pay of carers. This would stop families having to weigh up the costs of going out to work and it would mean that parents did not have an interest in keeping the pay of carers as low as possible. Such a childcare system would cost money but probably not as much as it seems. Other European countries provide substantially more, cheaper care than Britain does. They count the benefits in terms of women's workforce participation. The Daycare Trust also estimates that any money spent on childcare will actually create larger savings later on because of improvements in children's performance in school, increased parental participation in work, reductions in crime and benefits for community renewal.[8]

Thinking about cleanliness, dirt and housework

Widespread, affordable childcare would help parents combine work with having a family and would make many people's lives more bearable, but it is not going to get the washing up done or clean the bath. To address the demand for paid help with cleaning we need to ask different questions about who does housework, why and if they should. This means thinking about attitudes towards dirt and cleanliness and towards housework and the meaning of home. We need to question whether the people who currently do most housework – women and the poor – should do it and whether that much cleaning really needs to be done.

The first of these questions is easy to answer. There is no reason why women should do more housework than men and there is no good reason why poor women in particular should be ghettoized in cleaning work. The creation of dirt is a perfectly natural process; something that we are all responsible for and something that we should all take responsibility for dealing with. There needs to be a general adjustment of attitudes so that dealing with dirt is no longer seen as demeaning but rather is thought of as laudable and necessary. No one wants a polluted water system, so we need to appreciate the people who deal with sewage. Likewise, the cleaning of personal dirt from clothes and houses should not be seen as low-status work.

In addition, the assumption that women are responsible for housework and that this is inherently low in value because it is unpaid and because women do it, needs to be addressed. Women's assumed responsibility and natural aptitude for housework is a mainstay of their position in society more generally. Women not only do more work than men, if unpaid work is counted, and have less leisure, they find it more difficult to compete for certain types of work and are concentrated in sectors that are related to their traditional domestic roles, all because of their implicit commitment to housework. Some women see hiring a cleaner as a solution if their male partner will not do his fair share around the house. But this is not a solution at all. It does not challenge the assumptions underlying the man's behaviour, it does not help the women who do just as much but cannot afford a cleaner and it certainly doesn't help their daughters to have better, more equal relationships in the future.

As well as challenging the enduring gender divisions within the home, another way to address the problem of too much housework and too little time is just not to do it, or at least, not to do it as much. Perhaps one solution is to give up pretending that we can do it all and just to let standards change. In particular we should stop judging people on the appearance of their houses. Maybe a family home that only gets vacuumed from time to time, has toys and other things not put away and doesn't have matching net curtains throughout is not proof that the occupiers are slovenly, or that the mother cannot cope. Maybe we should realize that it is just a sign that all the occupants have found something better to do with their lives than worry about cleaning.

If we stop judging people on the appearance of their homes we will also address the wastefulness of lifestyles that are organized to display wealth and status to others and that use the labour of domestic workers to do this. In a world with so many people in need, we should be appalled at houses designed meticulously to flaunt the cultural and economic assets of their inhabitants, to show their affluence and taste. People devote their whole lives to honing their homes into perfect showrooms and waste other people's lives making sure they are kept that way. There are domestic workers who are employed to clean floors with toothbrushes, to press three bathrobes for one person everyday and even to flush their employers' toilets for them![9] No one needs to live like that. The inequality that allows some people to pay others to clean up after them is not something that should be flaunted, it is something that should be fought against.

The growth of domestic employment in twenty-first century Britain is not a return to Victorian ways of living, it is the result of very modern and very global processes that affect the ways we organize our lives. If the words of optimistic historians two decades ago are going to be realized, and the age of domestic service is really going to come to an end, we will need a much fairer world than the one we currently live in. We will also need to change our attitudes towards dirt and cleaning and towards the role of women in the home. We will need to challenge the predominance that work has taken in so many people's lives and we will need to ensure working hours are reduced and the expectations put on workers for flexibility are kept in check. Perhaps the first step towards this better way of life is good socialized childcare for all children. Childcare that is flexible, affordable, accessible and high quality: care that parents have confidence in and where carers are fairly rewarded. This would begin to address the imbalance between families without work and families with too much. It would ensure workers' pay reflected their value, not their employer's income, and it would offer all families the prospect of a less stressful balance between work and home.

Notes

1 What is the servant problem?

1 Platt (2001).
2 Henshall Momsen (1999), p. 9.
3 Franks (2000), p. 108.
4 Reported in *Children Now*, 1–7 December 2004, pp. 18–19.
5 My own research was described by one journalist as 'trivia and political correctness' and while histories of domestic labour are now quite fashionable, historians have had trouble getting their work taken seriously in the past.
6 Quoted in the *Oxford Dictionary of Quotations* (1979), Third Edition, p. 497: 40.
7 Quoted in Davidson (1982), p. 171.
8 Republished 2003 by Hesperus Press, London.
9 Swift (2003), p. 60–1.
10 Dawes (1989), p. 18.
11 Davidson (1982), footnote, p. 181.
12 Anonymous (1899/2002).
13 Anonymous (1913/2002).
14 Quoted in Dawes (1983), p. 21.
15 Ibid., p. 167.
16 Davidson (1982), p. 179.

2 Caring in the new world order

1 Pink (1998); Horn (2004), pp. 36–53.
2 McBride (1976).
3 Horn (2004), pp. 30–5.
4 McBride (1976).
5 Hondagneu-Sotelo (2001), pp. 16–17.
6 Anonymous (1913/2002), p. 65.
7 Walter (2001), p. 144–7.
8 Platt (2001), p. 26.

9 Anderson (2000).

10 Quoted in Anderson (2000), p. 29.

11 Hinsliff (2003).

12 Anderson (2000), p. 23.

13 Quoted in Anderson (1993), p. 32.

14 Kofman *et al.* (2000), p. 131.

15 Anderson (1993), p. 32–4.

16 Ibid., p. 36.

17 Ibid., pp. 36–40.

18 Pratt (1999a).

19 Henshall Momen (1999).

20 Advertisement from the *Philippine Daily Enquirer* reproduced in Anderson (1993).

21 See Henshall Momsen (1999), Pratt (1999b), Stiell and England (1999).

22 Hondagneu-Sotelo (2001).

23 See Radcliffe (1990), Gill (1994).

24 Henshall Momsen (ed.) (1999), p. 81.

25 Anderson (2000), pp. 80–1.

26 Barbič and Miklavčič-Brezigar (1999).

27 Katz (2000).

28 Kofman *et al.* (2000), p. 131.

29 'Nurse shortage threatens NHS' BBC News 19 February 2002, http://news.bbc. co.uk/1/hi/health/1827487.stm. 'UK poaching South African Nurses' BBC News 9 December 2002, http://news.bbc.co.uk/1/hi/programmes/4×4_reports/ 2558445.stm.

30 Raghuram and Kofman (2002).

31 Tam (1999).

32 Constable (2003), p. 120.

33 Yeoh and Huang (1999a, 1999b).

34 Pratt (1997, 1999a).

35 Bakan and Stasiulis (eds) (1997), p. 7.

36 See Chang (2000), and Hondagneu-Sotelo (2001).

37 Mattingly (1999), p. 76.

38 Cabreros-Sud (1993).

39 Phizacklea (ed.) (1983), p. 98.

40 Quoted in Anderson (2000), p. 89.

41 See Kalayaan http://www.ourworld.compuserve.com/homepages/kalayaan/ home.htm.

42 See Anderson (2000), Chapter 6 for a history of the campaign.

43 When the research was being carried out these countries included all of the European Economic Area and Andorra, Bosnia-Herzegovina, Croatia, Cyprus, the Czech Republic, the Faeroes, Greenland, Hungary, Liechtenstein, Macedonia, Malta, Monaco, San Marino, Slovak Republic, Slovenia, Switzerland and Turkey. In December 2002 Poland, Estonia, Latvia, Lithuania, Bulgaria and Romania joined the scheme because of government concern that a greater supply of au pairs was needed (Addley (2002)).

44 See the Home Office web site: http://www.ind.homeoffice.gov.uk/default. asp?pageID=110 for the official outline of the scheme.

45 The Immigration Advisory Service, http://www.iasuk.org/advice/ searchdocument.asp?DocID=306, accessed 22 August 2003.

3 'Carefree' Britain

1 Office of National Statistics (2003a), p. 394.

2 Duffield (2002).

3 Hakim (1994).

4 Duffield (2002).

5 Ibid.

6 Ibid., Table 4, p. 615.

7 Hamnett (2003), Table 4.1, p. 80.

8 Franks (2000), p. 67.

9 Ibid., p. 69.

10 Ibid., p. 70.

11 Leach (1994), p. 16.

12 Hochschild (2000), p. 92.

13 Massey (1995).

14 Daycare Trust (2000).

15 Franks (2000), p. 108.

16 Office of National Statistics (2003b).

17 Office of National Statistics (2003c).

18 Franks (2000), p. 68–9.

19 Hogath *et al.* (2001), p. 372.

20 Branigan (2002).

21 Hochschild (2000), p. 67.

22 Ibid., p. 178–9.

23 Gregson and Lowe (1994).

24 Ehrenreich (2003), p. 89–90.

25 Harvey (2000), p. 42–3.

26 Ibid., p. 44.

27 Ehrenreich (2003), p. 85.

28 Inland Revenue (2003).

29 This was found in a survey in Gregson and Lowe (1994). It was also reiterated in interviews with employment agencies placing domestic workers throughout the country.

30 Hamnett (2003), p. 207.

31 Ibid., Table 4.11, p. 96.

32 Ibid., pp. 91–3.

33 Ibid., Chapter 8, especially Table 8.2. Family Credit and Income Support are government benefits paid to households who have very low earnings or are out of work but not entitled to benefits such as Jobseekers Allowance, for example lone parents caring for their children. Housing Benefit is paid towards the cost of rent

for those with very low incomes, normally people on benefits or state pensions.
34 Ehrenreich (2003), p. 85.
35 See Williams and Windebank (1994, 1995).
36 See also Watt (2003) and Gregson and Lowe (1994).
37 Ibid., p. 1785.
38 Hamnett (2003), p. 73.
39 Courture Concierge service, http://www.courture.co.uk/index.asp?source=adwords&campaignname=concierge
40 *The Which? Guide to Domestic Help* (1998), quoted in Anderson (2000), p. 86.
41 McClimont (2002).
42 Ibid.
43 Coomans (2002).
44 McClimont (2002).

4 Minding the gaps: the crisis in childcare

1 Daycare Trust (2003b).
2 Leach (1994), p. 6.
3 Fincher (1996), p. 146.
4 Joshi and Davis (1992).
5 Randall and Fisher (1999).
6 Daycare Trust (2001).
7 Roberts (2002).
8 Daycare Trust (2002c), p. 4.
9 Figures calculated by the Inland Revenue Working Tax Credit Helpline.
10 Daycare Trust (2003b).
11 Daycare Trust (2001), p. 2.
12 Roberts (2003).
13 Daycare Trust (2002a).
14 Daycare Trust (2003a).
15 Daycare Trust (2002a).
16 Carvel (2003).
17 Daycare Trust (2005).
18 Carvel (2004).
19 For details see http://www.surestart.gov.uk/.
20 DfES (2002b).
21 Daycare Trust (2001).
22 Marchbank (2000).
23 Daycare Trust (2002b), p. 3.
24 Daycare Trust (2002b), pp. 1–2.
25 Daycare Trust (2003a).
26 Pullinger and Summerfield (eds) (1998), Table 3.22, p. 39.
27 Government Statistical Service (1998), pp. 179–83.
28 This phrase comes from work by Helen Jarvis of the University of Newcastle-upon-Tyne.

29 Government Statistical Service (1998), pp. 179–83.
30 Daycare Trust (2000).
31 Daycare Trust (2002c).
32 Department for Education and Skills (2002a).
33 Daycare Trust (2003b), p. 1.
34 Daycare Trust (2001), p. 4.
35 Quoted in Franks (2000), p. 80.
36 Hochschild (1997), p. 97, p. 278 (note 1, Chapter 7).
37 Roberts (2002).
38 Flanagan (2002).
39 See Flanagan (2002) and www.norland.co.uk.

5 The new Upstairs, Downstairs

 1 Sambrook (2002).
 2 See Sambrook (2002) and Dawes (1989).
 3 Parry (2003).
 4 Sambrook (2002), p. 69.
 5 Horn (2004), p. 44.
 6 Sambrook (2002), p. 100.
 7 Parry (2003).
 8 *The Lady*, 23 December 2003 to 5 January 2004, p. 90.
 9 *The Lady*, 20 to 26 January 2004, p. 81.
10 See also Anderson (2003), p. 105.
11 The wages for housework campaign argued that women should be paid a wage
    by the government for the work that they did. See Malos (ed.) (1995).
12 Quoted in Anderson (2000), pp. 91–2.
13 See Anderson (1993).
14 Zarembka (2003).
15 Kraus and McLaughlin (2002).
16 Sambrook (2002), p. 222.

6 A life between slavery and luxury: living as a domestic worker

 1 See Anderson (2000) for examples in Europe, Hondagneu Sotelo (2001) for the
    USA, Chaney and Garcia Castro (eds) (1989), for Latin America and the Carib-
    bean, and Henshall Momsen (ed.) (1999) for examples from a range of
    countries.
 2 See Gregson and Lowe (1994).
 3 Department for Transport and Industry (2004).
 4 Kraus and McLaughlin (2002).
 5 Employment law does apply to all employees, whether or not they are formally
    employed. However, au pairs are not considered to be employees and therefore

are not covered by specific employment legislation. A home is not considered by law to be a workplace and therefore certain aspects of employment law, including elements of health and safety protection, do not apply to any domestic workers, which is rather a scandal to my mind.

6 Personal communication from a key worker at Kalyaaan.

7 A number of academic writers have discussed the ambivalent nature of integration within an employers' family and the increased work that can result from it. See for example Gregson and Lowe (1994) for a detailed discussion of false kin relations within households employing nannies and cleaners in Britain; Hondagneu- Sotelo (2001) for the United States, England and Stiell (1997) for Canada, Young (1987) on Latin America and Cox and Narula (2003) for more detail on au pairs in London.

8 Taylor (1976).

9 Ibid., p. 14.

10 This was an instruction given to housemaids, quote in Sambrook (2002), p. 100.

11 See for example, Anderson (2001), Bakan and Stasiulis (eds) (1997), p. 7, and Hondagneu-Sotelo (2001).

7 Conclusion: solving the servant problem

1 Taylor (1976).

2 See Parreñas (2001), for a particularly detailed discussion of informal gatherings amongst domestic workers in Italy.

3 See papers in Chaney and Garcia Castro (eds) (1989).

4 See the Professional Association of Teachers web site, www.pat.org.uk.

5 See Anderson (2000), Chapter 6 for a history of this campaign and also Anderson (2001).

6 Gregson and Lowe (1994).
See amongst many others examples in Hondagneu-Sotelo (2001), Gill (1994), Radcliffe (1990) and Young (1987).

7 Anderson (2002), Part 2, pp. 29–30.

8 Daycare Trust (2002c).

9 These example are from interviews with domestic workers by Bridget Anderson. One domestic worker explained 'Every day I clean for my madam one pair of riding shoes, two pairs of walking shoes, house shoes. That is every day, just for one person. . . . Plus the children: that's one pair of rubbers and one pair of school shoes . . . Fourteen pairs of shoes every day. My time is already finished . . . You will be wondering why she has so many bathrobes, one silk and two cotton. I say Why does Madam have so many bathrobes? Everyday you have to hang them up. Everyday you have to press the back because it is crumpled.' See Anderson (2003), pp. 105 and 107.

References

Addley, Esther (2002) 'Not quite Mary Poppins', *Guardian G2*, 28 November 2002 pp. 1–3.

Anderson, Bridget (1993) *Britain's Secret Slaves*, London: Anti-Slavery International and Kalayaan.

Anderson, Bridget (2000) *Doing the Dirty Work: The Global Politics of Domestic Labour*, London: Zed Books.

Anderson, Bridget (2001) 'Different roots in common ground: transnationalism and migrant domestic workers in London', *Journal of Ethnic and Migration Studies* 24(4): pp. 673–83.

Anderson, Bridget (2003) 'Just another job? The commodification of domestic labour', in Ehrenreich, Barbara and Hochschild, Arlie Russell (eds) *Global Woman: Nannies, Maids and Sex Workers in the New Economy*, London: Granta Books, pp. 104–14.

Anderson, Bridget and O'Connell Davidson, Julia (2002) *The Demand Side of Trafficking? A Multi-Country Pilot Study* Stockholm: Save the Children Sweden.

Anonymous (1899/2002) *Appearances and How to Keep Them Up on a Limited Income*, East Grinstead, Sussex: Copper Beech Publishing.

Anonymous (1913/2002) *The Servantless Household: How to Cope, Some Polite Advice*, East Grinstead, Sussex: Copper Beech Publishing.

Bakan, Abigail and Stasiulis, Daiva (eds) (1997) *Not One of the Family: Foreign Domestic Workers in Canada*, Toronto: University of Toronto Press.

Barbič, Ana and Miklavčič-Brezigar, Inga (1999) 'Domestic work abroad: a necessity and an opportunity for rural women from the Goriška borderland region of Slovenia', in Henshall Momsen, J. (ed.) (1999) *Gender, Migration and Domestic Service*, pp. 164–77.

Branigan, Tania (2002) 'Earnings of women still lag by 18%', *Guardian*, 3 June 2002.

Cabreros-Sud, Veena (1993) 'New York Times on immigrants: give us your healthy, wealthy and 24-hour nannies', www.fair.org/extra/9304/nyt-immigration.html, accessed 18/08/2003.

Carvel, John (2003) 'Childcare grows into £2.15bn business: nurseries bloom despite low pay', *Guardian*, 6 May 2003.

Carvel, John (2004) 'Women workers earn £500 less a month than men says EOC', *Guardian*, 14 January 2004.

Chang, Grace (2000) *Disposable Domestics: Immigrant Women Workers in the Global Economy*, Cambridge, MA: South End Press.

Constable, Nicole (2003) 'Filipina workers in Hong Kong homes: household rules and relations', in Ehrenreich, Barbara and Hochschild, Arlie Russell (eds) *Global Woman: Nannies, Maids and Sex Workers in the New Economy*, London: Granta Books, pp. 115–41.

Coomans, Gerry (2002) 'Labour supply in European context: demographic determinants and competence issues', paper given at 'Care Workers – Matching Supply and Demand: a European Conference on Employment Issues in the Care of Children and Older People Living at Home', 20–21 June 2002, Sheffield Hallam University, Sheffield, UK.

Cox, Rosie and Narula, Rekha (2003) 'Playing happy families: rules and relationships in au pair employing households', *Gender, Place and Culture* 10(4): 333–44.

Davidson, Caroline (1982) *A Woman's Work is Never Done: A History of Housework in the British Isles 1650–1959*, London: Chatto and Windus.

Dawes, Frank Victor (1983) *Not in Front of the Servants A True Portrait of Upstairs Downstairs Life*, London: Random House in association with the National Trust.

Daycare Trust (2000) *No More Nine to Five: Childcare in a Changing World*, London: The Daycare Trust.

Daycare Trust (2001) *The Price Parents Pay: Sharing the Costs of Childcare*, London: The Daycare Trust.

Daycare Trust (2002a) 'New statistics show childcare gap remains at one place for every seven children under eight', http://www.gn.apc.org/womeninlondon/dct-0725.htm, accessed 03/02/2002.

Daycare Trust (2002b) *Older and Bolder: A New Approach to Creating Out of School Services for 10 to 14 year Olds*, London: The Daycare Trust.

Daycare Trust (2002c) *Raising Expectations: Delivering Childcare for All*, London: The Daycare Trust.

Daycare Trust (2003a) 'Parents need more help from government and employers as childcare bill rockets', http://www/womeninlondon.org.uk/dct-302.htm, accessed 19/05/2003.

Daycare Trust (2003b) *Making Childcare Work*, London: The Daycare Trust.

Daycare Trust (2005) 'Parents pay inflation-busting costs of childcare', http://www.daycaretrust.org.uk/article.php?sid=245

Department for Education and Skills (2002a) 'Provision for children under five years of age in England, January 2001', *The Department for Education and Skills Statistical Bulletin* http://www.dfes.gov.uk/statistics/DB/SBU/b0300/227-t1.htm, accessed 02/02/2002.

Department for Education and Skills (2002b) Statistical Bulletin, Table 1, http://www.dfes.gov.uk/statistics/DB/SBU/bo300/227-t1.htm, accessed 03/02/2002.

Department for Transport and Industry (2004) *A Detailed Guide to the National Minimum Wage*, http://www.dti.gov.uk/er/nmw/gtmw.pdf.

Duffield, Melanie (2002) 'Trends in female employment 2002', *Labour Market Trends*, November: 605–16.

Ehrenreich, Barbara (2003) 'Maid to order', in Ehrenreich, Barbara and Hochschild, Arlie Russell (eds) *Global Woman: Nannies, Maids and Sex Workers in the New Economy*, London: Granta Books, pp. 85–103.

England, Kim and Stiell, Bernadette (1997) ' "They think you're as stupid as your English is": constructing foreign domestic workers in Toronto', *Environment and Planning A* 29: 195–215.

Fincher, Ruth (1996) 'The state and childcare: an international review from a geographical perspective', in England, Kim (ed.) *Who Will Mind the Baby: Geographies of Childcare and Working Mothers*, London: Routledge, pp. 143–69.

Flanagan, Ben (2002) 'Nannies', *Observer*, 17 March 2000.

Franks, Suzanne (2000) *Having None of It: Women, Men and the Future of Work*, London: Granta Books.

Gill, Lesley (1994) *Precarious Dependencies: Gender, Class and Domestic Service in Bolivia*, New York: Columbia University Press.

Government Statistical Service (1998) *Living in Britain: Results from the 1998 General Household Survey*, London: Office of National Statistics.

Gregson, Nicky and Lowe, Michelle (1994) *Servicing the Middle Classes: Class, Gender and Waged Domestic Labour in Contemporary Britain*, London: Routledge.

Hakim, Catherine (1994) 'The myth of rising female employment', *Work, Employment and Society* 7(1): 97–120.

Hamnett, Chris (2003) *Unequal City: London in the Global Arena*, London: Routledge.

Harvey, David (2000) *Spaces of Hope*, Edinburgh: Edinburgh University Press.

Henshall Momsen, Janet (1999) *Gender, Migration and Domestic Service*, London: Routledge.

Hinsliff, Gaby (2003) 'Children forced into UK slavery: hidden secret of African girls smuggled as drudges', *Observer*, 18 May 2003.

Hochschild, Arlie Russell (1997) *The Time Bind: When Work Becomes Home and Home Becomes Work*, New York: Henry, Holt.

Hogath, Terence, Hasluck, Chris, Pierre, Gaelle, Winterbotham, Mark and Vivian, David (2001) 'Work-life balance 2000: Results from the baseline study', *Labour Market Trends* July.

Hondagneu-Sotelo, Pierrette (2001) *Doméstica: Immigrant Workers Cleaning and Caring in the Shadows of Affluence*, Berkeley: University of California Press.

Horn, Pamela (2004) *The Rise and Fall of the Victorian Servant*, Sparkford: Sutton Publishing.

Inland Revenue (2003) 'Share of the wealth: 1% of the population owns 22% of wealth', National Statistics Online, www.statistics.gov.uk/cci/nugget.asp?id=2, accessed 17/09/2003.

Joshi, Heather and Davis, Hugh (1992) *Childcare and Mothers' Lifetime Earnings: Some European Contrasts*, London: Centre for Economic Policy Research, Discussion Paper 600.

Katz, Cindy (2000) 'Vagabond capitalism and the necessity of social reproduction', *Antipode* 33: 709–28.

Kofman, Eleonore, Phizacklea, Annie, Raghuram, Parvati and Sales, Rosemary (2000) *Gender and International Migration in Europe: Employment, Welfare and Politics*, London: Routledge.

Kraus, Nicola and McLaughlin, Emma (2002) *The Nanny Diaries*, London: Penguin Books.

Leach, Penelope (1994) *Children First! What our Society Must Do and is Not Doing for Children Today*, London: Michael Joseph.

McBride, Theresa (1976) *The Domestic Revolution: The Modernization of Household Service in England and France 1820–1920*, New York: Holmes and Meier.

McClimont, Bill (2002) 'Future labour supply issues', paper given at 'Care Workers – Matching Supply and Demand: a European Conference on Employment Issues in the Care of Children and Older People Living at Home', 20–21 June 2002, Sheffield Hallam University, Sheffield UK.

Malos, Ellen (ed.) (1995) *The Politics of Housework*, Cheltenham: New Clarion.

Marchbank, Jennifer (2000) *Women, Power and Policy: Comparative Studies of Childcare*, London: Routledge.

Massey, Doreen (1995) 'Masculinity, dualisms and high technology', *Transactions of the Institute of British Geographers* 20: 487–99.

Mattingly, Doreen (1999) 'Making maids: United States immigration policy and immigrant domestic workers', in Henshall Momsen, J. (ed.) (1999) *Gender, Migration and Domestic Service*, London: Routledge, pp. 62–80.

Momsen. See Henshall Momsen.

Office of National Statistics (2003a) *Labour Market Trends* August.

Office of National Statistics (2003b) 'Jobs about the house: household chores still women's work?', UK 2000 Time Use Survey, published 30 January 2003 at http://www.statistics.gov.uk/CCI/nugget.asp?ID=288.

Office of National Statistics (2003c) The UK 2000 Time Use Survey at http://www.statistics.gov.uk/timeuse/default.asp.

Parreñas, Rhacel (2001) *Servants of Globalization*, Stanford: Stanford University Press.

Parry, Ryan (2003) 'Our man in the Palace: my life as a footman', *Daily Mirror*, 19 November 2003.

Phizacklea, Annie (ed.) (1983) *One Way Ticket: Migration and Female Labour*, London: Routledge and Kegan Paul.

Pink, John (1998) *'Country Girls Preferred': Victorian Domestic Servants in the Suburbs*, Surbiton, Surrey: JRP.

Platt, Edward (2001) 'This is a serious business', *The Business: The Financial Times Magazine*, London, 20 October 2001, p. 26.

Pratt, Geraldine (1997) 'Stereotypes and ambivalence: the construction of domestic workers in Vancouver, British Columbia', *Gender, Place and Culture* 4(2): 159–77.

Pratt, Geraldine (1999a) 'From registered nurse to registered nanny: discursive geographies of Filipina domestic workers in Vancouver B.C.', *Economic Geography* 75(3): 215–36.

Pratt, Geraldine (1999b) 'Is this Canada? Domestic workers' experiences in Vancouver, BC', in Henshall Momsen, Janet (ed.) (1999) *Gender, Migration and Domestic Service*, pp. 23–42.

Pullinger, John and Summerfield, Carol (eds) (1998) *Social Focus on Men and Women*, London: The Stationery Office.

Radcliffe, Sarah (1990) 'Ethnicity, patriarchy and incorporation into the nation: female migrants as domestic servants in Peru', *Environment and Planning D: Society and Space* 8, pp. 379–93.

Raghuram, Parvati and Kofman, Eleonore (2002) 'The state, skilled labour markets, and immigration: the case of doctors in England', *Environment and Planning A* 34, pp. 2071–89.

Randall, Vicky and Fisher, Kim (1999) *Towards Explaining Child Day Care Policy Variations Amongst the Local Authorities*, Colchester: ESRC Centre on Micro-Social Change.

Roberts, Yvonne (2002) 'Who's left holding the baby?' *Guardian*, 12 April 2002.

Roberts, Yvonne (2003) 'Are you tough enough?' *Observer*, 11 May 2003.

Sambrook, Pamela A. (2002) *The Country House Servant*, Stroud: Sutton Publishing with The National Trust.

Steill, Bernadette and England, Kim (1999) 'Jamaican domestics, Filipina housekeepers and English nannies: representations of Toronto's foreign domestic workers', in Henshall Momsen, Janet (ed.) (1999) *Gender, Migration and Domestic Service*, pp. 43–61.

Swift, Jonathan (2003) *Directions to Servants*, London: Hesperus Press.

Tam, Vicky C.W. (1999) 'Foreign domestic helpers in Hong Kong and their role in childcare provision', in Henshall Momsen, Janet (ed.) (1999) *Gender, Migration and Domestic Service*, pp. 263–76.

Taylor, Pam (1976) 'Women Domestic Servants 1919–1939: A Study of a Hidden Army, Illustrated by Servants' own Recollected Experiences', The University of Birmingham Centre for Contemporary Cultural Studies, Stencilled Occasional Papers.

Walter, Bronwen (2001) *Outsiders Inside: Whiteness, Place and Irish Women*, London: Routledge.

Watt, Paul (2003) 'Urban marginality and labour market restructuring: local authority tenant and employment in an inner London borough', *Urban Studies* 40: 1769–89.

Williams, Colin and Windebank, Jan (1994) 'Spatial variations in the informal sector: a review of evidence from the European Union', *Regional Studies* 28: 819–25.

Williams, Colin and Windebank, Jan (1995) 'Social polarization of households in contemporary Britain: a "whole economy" perspective', *Regional Studies* 29: 727–32.

Yeoh, Brenda, and Huang, Shirlena (1999a) 'Spaces at the margins: migrant domestic workers and the development of civil society in Singapore', *Environment and Planning A* 31: 1149–67.

Yeoh, Brenda and Huang, Shirlena (1999b) 'Singapore women and foreign domestic workers: negotiating domestic work and motherhood.' In Henshall Momsen,

Janet (ed.)(1999) *Gender, Migration and Domestic Service,* London: Routledge, pp. 277–300.

Young, Grace (1987) 'The myth of being "just like a daughter"', *Latin American Perspectives* 14: 365–80.

Zarembka, Joy (2003) 'America's dirty work: migrant maids and modern-day slavery', in Ehrenreich, Barbara and Hochschild, Arlie Russell (eds) *Global Woman: Nannies, Maids and Sex Workers in the New Economy*, pp. 142–52.

Index